The Farmer's Wife
Baking Cookbook

Over 300 Blue Ribbon Recipes

Lela Nargi, Editor

Voyageur Press

First published in 2007 by Voyageur Press, an imprint of MBI Publishing Company LLC, Galtier Plaza, Suite 200, 380 Jackson Street, St. Paul, MN 55101 USA

Voyageur Press titles are also available at discounts in bulk quantity for industrial or sales-promotional use. For details write to Special Sales Manager at MBI Publishing Company, Galtier Plaza, Suite 200, 380 Jackson Street, St. Paul, MN 55101 USA.

To find out more about our books, join us online at www.voyageurpress.com.

ISBN-13: 978-0-7603-2923-8

Editor: Kari A. Cornell
Designers: Jennifer Bergstrom and Sara Holle

Printed in China

The farmer's wife baking cookbook : over 300 blue ribbon recipes / edited by Lela Nargi.
    p. cm.
  ISBN-13: 978-0-7603-2923-8 (ringbound)
  1. Baking. I. Nargi, Lela, 1967-
  TX765.F37 2007
  641.8'15—dc22
                                    2007004860

About the author:
Editor Lela Nargi is a writer who lives in Brooklyn, New York. She is the author of *Around the Table: Women on Food, Cooking, Nourishment, Love . . . and the Mothers Who Dished It Up for Them* and *Knitting Lessons: Tales from the Knitting Path*. She is also the editor of *Knitting Memories: Reflections on the Knitter's Life,* published by Voyageur Press in 2006.

Acknowledgments

I am grateful to *Farm Journal* for granting me permission to use text, art, and photos from *The Farmer's Wife* for the purpose of this cookbook.

To Kari Cornell and MBI Publishing for thinking I'd be right for this project.

To Rebecca J. Faille at King Arthur Flour, and Sandra Oliver of *Food History News,* for their invaluable research assistance.

To my mother for her good-natured copyediting and common sense.

And to Rob and Ada.

A warm-hearted kitchen

The **Heart** *of* **Good Living**

Contents

INTRODUCTION

*T*he *Farmer's Wife* was a monthly magazine published in Minnesota between 1893 and 1939. In an era long before the Internet and high-speed travel connected us all, the magazine aimed to offer community among hard-working rural women by providing a forum for their questions and concerns and assistance in the day-to-day goings on about the farm—everything from raising chickens and slaughtering hogs, to managing scant funds and dressing the children, to keeping house and running the kitchen.

The kitchen is where the farmer's wife really shone. And of all the various and important tasks she performed there, it was baking that allowed her the broadest arena for expression. She could be creative in the kitchen, letting her imagination run wild over cakes and cookies and pastries of her own invention. She could show off her skill, whipping up crisp-crusted breads and fine-crumb cakes of the utmost perfection. She could exercise one of the most esteemed qualities among country women—that of thrift, using the eggs, milk, butter, preserves, and other stores abundant on any farm—while at the same time showing love and care for her family through the delectable treats she offered them with and between each meal.

The farmer's wife baked for every circumstance and occasion. She baked all the family's bread, to accompany meals, to slice for sandwiches, and, when stale, to grind for crumbs. At a time when "dinner" was called "supper" and no supper was complete without dessert, she baked tarts and pastries to follow-up roasts and stews and casseroles. She baked cookies and cupcakes to stick in her children's lunch pails. She baked dainties and muffins to serve at afternoon teas and club luncheons. She baked elaborate cakes for birthdays and weddings. She baked simple pies in great profusion to serve at threshing parties and other large community gatherings. Through the rationing of World War I, the privations of the Great Depression, and the uncertainty of the years leading up to World War II, the farmer's wife baked what she had—sometimes absent wheat and sugar—and she baked it as well as she could.

Perhaps one of the most defining, and surprising, characteristics of the farmer's wife was her curiosity—about new techniques and also the world at large. Among the pages of this book you'll find many of the things you'd expect from the farmer's wife: cherry pies, sourdough bread, and layer cakes. But you'll also find recipes for such things as Cornish Pasties and Danish Krandse, because such things, from far-away lands, fascinated the farmer's wife, and expanded her baking universe, and often enough, reflected her own heritage; Vinegar Pie and Parkin, rarely to be found these days in baking books but once true stand-bys of the farm kitchen; and so-called Victory breads that use potatoes and cornmeal and other grains to replace or expand wheat flour, because they are poignant reminders of years past, and a testament to the durability and ingenuity of the farmer's wife.

The recipes have been reprinted here much as they appeared on the pages of the magazine. Most recipes have been taken from issues spanning 1911 to 1939, and many were written by the magazine's own readers. In their language, they reflect the curious style and manners of their times, and herein lies a great deal of their charm, and the reason I have chosen to alter them as little as possible. Anyone accustomed to reading cookbooks, and any habitual baker, will feel right at home among the pages of this book. After all, the farmer's wife was nothing if not common-sensical, and so were her recipes. Anyone new to cookbooks, and more particularly, historical cookbooks, is advised to follow the golden rule of the recipe: Read it thoroughly, start to finish and preferably more than once, before embarking. Make sure you understand the instructions and the order in which they are to be carried out; make sure you have all the ingredients at hand and assembled; and make sure to preheat your oven a good 20 to 30 minutes before you are ready to bake.

Wherever possible, I have attempted to abolish confusing, misleading, or laborious instructions. I've also substituted modern equivalents for obsolete measurements such as the gill (4 ounces), and the teacup (8 ounces). More than anything, this book wants to be used, not merely perused and admired. So, please use it! And know that as you do, you are baking up a bit of farmland history.

—*Lela Nargi*

BAKING INSURANCE

by
*Miriam
J.
Williams*

WHAT happens when the oven isn't right? If it is quite a bit off toward the too-hot or too-cool side, the result shows up in pale bread, heavy biscuits, soggy undercrusts, dry undersized cakes. How to avoid failures and disappointments in baking is every homemaker's wish.

There is always the crusader for *the one right way*, no other method is right. There is not necessarily one right way of baking a certain product, for experiments may show that several methods are reasonably successful. The vote of the majority, however, will be for one, or perhaps two, methods which are the most satisfactory with average conditions.

Personal opinion will always enter in, of course, as to which pie or cake or bread is the most satisfactorily baked. As for appearance, most judges vote for a fairly well-browned product. They want the sides and bottom of bread to be a medium brown, and the crust of pies at least lightly browned rather than pale in color. Correct baking is important for good texture and flavor, too, and in the eyes of the judge, these are more important than appearance. Usually the three go hand-in-hand, that which looks really good before it is cut is equally pleasing in texture and taste.

In the May issue of THE FARMER'S WIFE Magazine was an article on the importance of home baking in the farm woman's routine. Studies show that the average one is poorly equipped with baking guides, nor is she particularly time and temperature conscious. Suggestions were given as to the selection of

General Baking Rules

EGG AND CHEESE DISHES should be baked in a *slow* or *very moderate* oven, (protein foods are easily toughened by heat). Cakes containing many eggs, meringues, custards, souffles are baked slowly for this reason.

MEAT, CHICKEN AND FISH, which are also protein foods, are toughened by too-high heat, and there is also undesirable loss by shrinkage. They are best baked (roasted) in a *slow* or *moderate* oven. Exceptions are tender steaks, broilers or fish fillets, etc., which are first browned quickly or broiled in a *very hot* or *hot* oven.

QUICK BREADS should bake quickly, unless in loaf form. Muffins and cornbread require a *hot* oven while biscuits bake to good advantage in a *very hot* oven. Pop-overs and cream puffs need a *very hot* oven at the start, and a more *moderate* oven to finish baking. Yeast breads are baked in a *moderate* or *moderately hot* oven.

SUGARY FOODS or those containing

A BAKING GUIDE

Kind of Oven	Temperature	Use For
very slow	below 300° F.	Fruit Cakes, Baked Beans.
slow	300°—340° F.	Meringues, Sponge, Angel Cakes, Tender Uncovered Roasts, Some Loaf Cakes.
moderate	350°—390° F.	Most Cakes and Cookies, Most Baked Vegetable and Main Dishes, Braised Meats, Meat Loaf, Custards, Yeast Bread.
hot	400°—440° F.	Muffins, Corn Bread, Pop-Overs, Some Drop Cookies, Meat Pie, Some Filled Pies.
very hot	450° and over	Biscuits, Pie Shells, To Start Custard Pies, To Brown Toppings and Sear Meats.

The term *very moderate* is sometimes used to describe ovens not quite 350° in temperature. *Moderately hot* may be used to describe the range from 375° to 400° F.

Biscuits baked at 450° F. (outside), and 375° F. (center). Too slow an oven means less volume and rounding rather than squared-off top

Meringues baked at 375° F. (left) and between 300° and 325° F. (right). Too hot an oven means tough, over-browned and shrunken meringues. The same is true of pie meringue

Chocolate cake baked at 350° F. (left) and 400° F. (right). Too hot an oven made it peak, which when cooled flattened into a heavy streak, with less volume

baking pans, their placement in the oven and other important factors in baking. A reliable portable thermometer, preferably of the mercury type, was recommended as a wise investment for the woman who does not have a regulated oven. And here is a reasonable guide to baking temperatures and a brief explanation as to why these temperatures are good.

Any baking guide must be comparative, for it is a combination of time and temperature which gives the desired result. For example, a higher temperature than usually recommended may give a satisfactory bake if a shorter time is used, and wise is the cook who observes and notes these variations.

molasses or honey should bake in a *slow* or *moderate* oven to avoid burning. Fancy sweet rolls, gingerbread, molasses cookies and cakes and cookies containing honey come in this group. Fruit cakes are baked in a *very slow* oven because of their high percentage of candied or dried fruits and their thick form.

SMALL OR THIN PRODUCTS bake more quickly than large ones. For example, the oven for loaf cakes should be *slow* or *moderate* depending upon the kind of cake, and *moderate* or *moderately hot* for cup and layer cakes. Cakes and cookies with added richness in the way of fat, chocolate, eggs, and nuts bake more slowly than plain cakes. Exceptions are thin, rich cookies which are usually baked in a *hot* or *very hot* oven.

PASTRY requires a *hot* or *very hot* oven to make it crisp rather than soft and somewhat greasy. Empty pie shells should bake to a light brown in 10 to 12 minutes. Pies with fruit filling are baked in a *hot* oven; those with a custard filling are started in a *hot* or *very hot* oven and finished baking more slowly.

CASSEROLE DISHES, as scalloped vegetable and main dishes are usually baked in a *moderate* oven. If all ingredients are previously cooked, a *hot* oven for a shorter time is usually better.

HOW TO USE
THIS BOOK—
READ THIS FIRST

In any recipe, shortening can be substituted for lard. The word "fat" can be interpreted as "butter"—use accordingly.

Quite a number of the original *Farmer's Wife* baking recipes call for sour milk. According to Sandra Oliver, editor of *Food History News*, sour milk was a naturally occurring product on farms in the days of pre-pasteurization, and was very useful for baking. "The acidity in the sour milk interacted with the alkaline in the baking soda to make the gas that raised baked goods," she explains. I've substituted buttermilk in the recipes that call for sour milk. If you'd like to make your own sour milk, add 1 tbsp. vinegar to 1 c. "sweet" milk (a word the *Farmer's Wife* used to differentiate regular milk from "sour" milk).

References in the recipes to canned fruit almost always means fruit
canned by the farmer's wife herself. Either high-quality store-bought
canned fruit or fresh fruit can be substituted.

Always sift flour once before measuring.

1 pint = 2 c.
1 quart = 4 c.

1 pound yields:
4 c. sifted all-purpose flour
4½ c. sifted cake flour
3½ c. graham flour
3 c. cornmeal
5½ c. rolled oats
2¼ c. white sugar
2½ c. brown sugar
2¾ c. powdered sugar
1⅓ c. molasses or honey
2 c. milk
4 c. nut meats, chopped
3 c. dried fruit

Some recipes in this book do not stipulate exact oven temperatures. When in doubt, follow the chart below, and also these guidelines:
* Most cookies, cakes, and quick breads bake at 350°F.
* Most yeast breads bake at 375°F, and yeast rolls between 400°F and 425°F.
* Tarts bake at 375°F.

Oven temperatures:

Slow	Up to 300°F
Very moderate	300°F to 350°F
Moderate (Medium)	350°F to 400°F
Hot (Quick, Fast)	400°F to 450°F
Very hot (Very quick)	450°F to 500°F

Some recipes in this book do not stipulate baking times. The following guidelines can be used:

For cookies: bake until just golden.

For cakes: bake until the cake begins to pull away from the sides of the pan and a toothpick inserted in the center comes out clean.

For bread: bake until the bread begins to pull away from the sides of the pan and a toothpick inserted in the center comes out clean. Also tap the pan and listen for a hollow sound.

For custards: bake until just set.

For single-crust, filled pies: start in a hot oven (425°F to 450°F) for the first 10 minutes to crisp-up the crust, then lower the temperature to moderate (350°F) to finish.

For unfilled pie shells: bake at 425°F for 18 to 20 minutes, or until lightly brown.

For unfilled tart shells: bake at 425°F for 12 minutes.

COOKIES AND BARS

Say it with COOKIES

Say It with Cookies

December 1936

There's nothing quite like cookie baking day. Nothing quite so cheerful in its floury confusion as the cookie-day kitchen, or so compelling as the spicy smell when each pan comes from the oven. Nothing quite so absorbing to the cook as this task which keeps both hands busy and demands one watchful eye on the oven and another on the children making inroads on the freshly baked heap. And nothing quite so festive and Christmasy as a varied assortment of cookies packed as a gift.

Drop Cookies

Good Sugar Cookies

October 1911

2 eggs well beaten, 1 c. sugar and ½ c. lard, sugar and lard to be well creamed together. 5 tbsp. sour cream, the same of buttermilk, a pinch of salt, 1 tsp. baking powder, ½ tsp. baking soda, ½ tsp. each cinnamon and cloves, flour to make a soft dough (editor's note: use about 1½ to 2 cups, but start out with less and add as you go). Drop onto buttered baking sheets and bake in a hot oven (400°F).

—*Ida. L. Townsend*

Mrs. Sudduth's Cookies

December 1913

These cookies are delicious and when baked are very light. 1 c. sugar, ½ c. butter, 1 c. cream (sour cream may be used but if so use a small pinch of baking soda), 2 eggs, 2 tsp. baking powder, 2 tsp. vanilla, ½ tsp. lemon extract. Flour to make a very soft dough (editor's note: use about 1½ to 2 cups, but as with sugar cookies, start with less and increase as needed). Drop onto buttered cookie sheets and bake at 350°F.

Favorite Boston Cookies

February 1922

½ c. butter or other fat
¾ c. sugar
1 egg
1½ c. flour
1 tsp. baking powder
¼ tsp. salt
½ tsp. cinnamon
½ c. chopped raisins
¼ c. chopped walnut meats

Cream butter and add sugar slowly, creaming them together. Add well beaten egg. Sift 1 c. flour, baking powder, salt, and cinnamon together and add to egg mixture. Mix remainder of flour with the raisins and nuts and add. Mix thoroughly and drop from teaspoon 1 inch apart on flat greased pan. Bake in hot oven (400°F) 10 to 15 minutes. This makes about 36 cookies.

Eggless Cookies

November 1913

1 c. sugar
½ c. butter or shortening
½ c. sweet milk
½ tsp. baking soda

Drop onto unbuttered baking sheets and bake at 400°F. This recipe will be found convenient when cream and eggs are scarce. They will keep nice and tender for weeks.

—*Grace I. Henderson*

18

Bread Crumb Cookies

March 1927

1 c. bread crumbs
1 c. sugar
1 c. cream
½ c. butter
1 egg
½ c. raisins
½ tsp. cinnamon
½ tsp. cloves
1 tsp. vanilla
2 c. flour

Mix, drop on greased pans with a teaspoon, and bake in a moderate oven (350°F). Recipe makes 48.

—*Mrs. C.H., North Dakota*

A Drop Cookie (Bran)

August 1931

¼ c. butter
½ c. sugar
1 egg
½ c. raisins, or ¼ c. raisins and ¼ c. nuts
1 c. bran
¾ c. flour
1 tsp. baking powder
¼ tsp. salt
½ tsp. cinnamon
¼ tsp. ground cloves

Cream butter, add sugar, well beaten egg, raisins, and then bran and the remaining dry ingredients which have been sifted 3 times. Bake in a hot oven (400°F) for 20 minutes. Makes 15 cookies.

—*Mrs. D.D., Ohio*

Ginger Drop Cakes

October 1913

3 eggs; 1 c. each lard, molasses, and brown sugar; 1 large tbsp. powdered ginger; 1 tbsp. baking soda dissolved in 1 c. boiling water; 5 c. unsifted flour. Drop tablespoons of this mixture onto a slightly greased cookie sheet, about 3 inches apart. Bake at 350°F.

Lightening Drop Cakes

March 1916

¼ c. butter
2 eggs
sweet milk
1 c. sugar
1⅛ c. flour
2 tsp. baking powder

Melt the butter but do not let it become hot. Pour into a measuring cup, add the unbeaten eggs, fill to 1 c. with milk, and beat the contents of the cup 2 minutes with an egg beater. Add the sugar and beat again. Then add the flour, which has been mixed and sifted with the baking powder, and beat the whole mixture again. Drop onto buttered cookie sheets and bake at 350°F. Sprinkle finished cookies with powdered sugar.

Peanut Cookies

December 1936

½ c. fat
½ c. peanut butter
1 c. brown sugar
1 egg
½ tsp. salt
1⅔ c. flour
1 tsp. baking powder
½ tsp. baking soda
½ c. milk
1 c. chopped salted peanuts

Cream fat and peanut butter, add brown sugar and cream until fluffy. Add egg, beat thoroughly, then add sifted dry ingredients alternately with milk. Divide dough in half and to one lot add half of the chopped peanuts. Drop by spoonfuls on greased tin. Drop out the other half of dough in small spoonfuls, stamp down with glass covered with a damp cloth. Sprinkle with nuts. Bake in a moderately hot oven (375°F) about 10 to 12 minutes. This recipe makes 60 cookies. If brown-coated salted nuts are used, put in a salt sack and rub to remove husks. Fan out husks by pouring from one pan to another in the wind.

Rich Peanut Butter Cookies

November 1934

½ c. lard
½ c. butter
1 c. white sugar
1 c. brown sugar
1 c. peanut butter
2 eggs, beaten
3 c. flour
1 tsp. baking soda
½ tsp. salt
1 tsp. vanilla

Cream fats and sugars, then add peanut butter and mix well. Add eggs, then dry ingredients, sifted together, and vanilla. Mix well and shape in balls. Place about 2 inches apart on sheet and press 2 ways with a fork to flatten and mark. Bake in a moderate oven (375°F) until delicately browned.

Honey Hermits
1934

1⅓ c. strained honey (editor's note: "Strained" refers merely to honey that has been filtered of wax particles. Any store bought honey not in the comb will do.)
½ c. fat
1 tsp. cinnamon
½ tsp. cloves
½ tsp. nutmeg
1 egg, beaten
3 to 3½ c. flour
½ tsp. salt
¾ tsp. baking soda in ¼ c. water
1 c. chopped raisins, or ½ c. each nuts and raisins

Heat honey and fat together. Add spices to the mixture while it is hot. Cool and add egg. Alternately add flour and salt, sifted together, and baking soda in water, then raisins. Beat well. Drop on greased pans and bake in moderate oven (375°F) until brown.

Chocolate Honey Rounds
December 1936

½ c. fat
⅓ c. sugar
⅔ c. honey
2 eggs
2 squares melted unsweetened chocolate, left to cool slightly
3 c. sifted flour
½ to 1 tsp. ground anise
½ tsp. baking soda
1½ tsp. baking powder
½ tsp. salt
2 or 3 tbsp. cream

Cream fat, add sugar and honey, then eggs and cooled melted chocolate. Mix until very creamy. Add sifted dry ingredients and a little cream to blend. Shape into balls, place on a greased sheet and stamp into rounds by flattening with a glass covered with a damp cloth. Bake 10 minutes in a moderate oven (350°F). These are better after storing a few days in a covered tin.

Cocoanut Brownies

January 1914

1 c. buttermilk
1 c. molasses
1 c. light brown sugar
1 egg
piece of butter the size of an egg,
1 tsp. baking soda dissolved in milk
3⅓ c. flour
2 c. grated unsweetened cocoanut.

Combine all ingredients. Drop with teaspoon on buttered tins a little way apart.

Variation:
One can use raisins instead of cocoanut.

—Mrs. A.L.H., Illinois

Chocolate Drop Cookies

October 1932
(52 Cookies)

1 egg, well beaten
1 c. brown sugar
½ c. shortening, softened
2 squares unsweetened chocolate, melted
1½ c. flour
1/4 tsp. salt
2 tsp. baking soda
1½ tsp. baking powder
½ c. buttermilk
½ tsp. vanilla
½ c. nuts

Combine egg, sugar, shortening, and chocolate. Beat well.
Add sifted dry ingredients, liquids, and nuts. Mix thoroughly.
Drop from a teaspoon on a greased pan about an inch apart.
Bake in a moderate oven (350°F) about 15 minutes.

Note: ¾ c. whole wheat flour may be substituted for ½ of the white flour.

Spiced Oatmeal Cookies

1934

Only the *best* Raisins could make these cookies so *good!*

That old stand-by, with variations

1 c. shortening (½ lb.)
2 c. brown sugar
2 eggs
1 c. buttermilk
2½ c. flour
1 tsp. baking soda
¾ tsp. salt
3 tsp. mixed spice (taken from a mixture made from 4 tbsp. cinnamon, 2 tbsp. nutmeg, and 2 tbsp. ground allspice or cloves)
2 c. rolled oats
2 c. raisins

Cream shortening with sugar. Beat eggs and mix with buttermilk. Mix flour well with baking soda, salt, and spices, and then with the rolled oats and raisins. Add liquid and dry ingredients alternately to the creamed shortening and sugar. Drop on greased pans and bake about 15 minutes in moderate oven (375°F). This makes 4 dozen large cookies. Divide in half for smaller amount.

Variations:
Use 3 c. whole wheat flour instead of white flour.
Use a scant cup of sweet milk instead of buttermilk; decrease baking soda to ½ tsp.; add 2 tsp. baking powder.
Grind rolled oats and raisins to get a finer texture.
Substitute bran for oats for a bran drop cookie. (editor's note: Oat bran flour can be purchased at health and kitchen specialty stores, and some supermarkets.)
Add 1 c. chopped nuts.

Coconut Flake Macaroon

April 1931

2 egg whites
1 c. sugar
1 c. shredded coconut
1 tbsp. flour
½ c. chopped nuts
2 c. crisp corn flakes
1 tsp. vanilla

Beat eggs, add sugar, coconut, flour, nuts, corn-flakes, and vanilla. Drop by spoonfuls on buttered pans. Bake in moderate oven (350°F) until lightly golden. Serves 30.

Oatmeal Macaroons

March 1910

Put ¼ cup of rolled oats into a bowl and cover it with 1 egg and 2 tbsp. each of cream, milk, and water, or 3 tbsp. rich milk. (editor's note: rich milk is equivalent to un-homogenized, creamline milk—where the cream rises to the surface—which is available at some health food stores and farmer's markets. Be sure to shake the milk well before use.) Let it stand until the oats have soaked up all the moisture, then add 1 c. powdered sugar, 1 tbsp. melted butter, and a little cinnamon. Sift 2 tsp. baking powder with 1 cup of flour and add it to the mixture with enough additional flour to make a stiff dough. Shape into balls as large as walnuts and bake in a moderate oven (350°F).

Meringues Glacées

April 1931

¾ c. water
2 c. sugar
5 egg whites
¼ tsp. salt
1 tsp. flavoring extract of your choosing

Heat the water and sugar in a smooth saucepan and stir until it boils, using a wooden spoon. Never stir after it boils and regulate the flame so that the syrup cooks evenly all over the pan. Cook until it reaches the soft ball stage (234°F to 240°F registered on a candy thermometer).

Let the syrup stand on stove until you beat the egg whites to stiff froth. Then add syrup slowly to eggs, beating until meringue is cold. Stir in flavoring. Drop on wax or parchment paper from teaspoon for small ones. Bake one hour in slow oven (250°F). The above recipe makes 12 shells. They may also be shaped with a pastry bag and made into rounds the size of mushroom caps and in short upright pieces like mushroom stems. Put caps and stems together while hot. Use 2 shells for each person, putting ice cream (½ c.) between the two. Garnish with whipped cream. Top with maraschino cherries.

Table Talk
For the Country Cookie Jar

Clara E. Wells, October 1914

Walnut Cookies

½ cupful walnut meats, cupful of buttermilk, teaspoonful of baking soda, quart and a half of flour, 3 eggs, 2 cupfuls of sugar.

Mix, drop onto greased baking sheets, and bake at 350°F.

Caraway Cookies

1 cupful of sweet milk, 1 cupful of butter, 1 teaspoonful of baking powder, ½ cup of caraway seeds, 2 cupfuls of maple sugar, quart and a half of flour. Roll thin and bake in a quick oven (400°F).

Harvest Ginger Cookies

1 pint of Orleans molasses, cupful of lard or butter, cupful of sugar, cupful of buttermilk, teaspoonful of baking soda, 2 quarts of flour. Roll and bake in a quick oven (400°F). They will disappear quickly when served at afternoon lunch in the harvest field.

Rolled Cookies

* Bouquets and Cookies *

May 1930

Five Minnesota women had just been publicly recognized as Master Farm Homemakers. In turn, each was expressing her appreciation of the honor and talking to the friends assembled.

Said Mrs. Charles E. Wirt of Lewiston: "I did not plan to be a farmer's wife. When we arrived at our new farm home we did not find the ordinary congratulations. It was all sympathy for my husband. My friends offered me the same sympathy. As we came to our front door we found tied to the knob a *Buckeye Cook Book* and a year's subscription to *The Farmer's Wife*. In that *Farmer's Wife* I found a recipe for sour cream cookies which I tried. It was the only real success in baking that I had that year. I thought perhaps readers of *The Farmer's Wife* would like that recipe I tried 20 years ago."

So we present the recipe. Here's luck to all of the 1930 farm brides, and may they find us as helpful a friend as did Mrs. Wirt years ago when the sour cream cookies made their debut!

Sour Cream Cookies

2 tbsp. shortening
2 c. white sugar
2 tbsp. butter
2 eggs
1 c. sour cream
flour
1 tsp. baking soda
1 tsp. baking powder

Cream shortening, add sugar and mix well with butter, add well beaten eggs, sour cream, and 2 c. of flour with leavening sifted in (our method). Add enough additional flour to make a soft dough. Roll and cut and bake in a hot oven (400°F).

Like the Ones Mother Used to Make
October 1914

1 cupful sour cream, ½ cupful butter, 1½ cupfuls of sugar, 3 eggs, 1 teaspoonful baking soda, flour enough to roll.

Mix, roll out, and bake at 350°F.

Sour Cream Cocoa Cookies
1934

1 egg, beaten light
1 c. sugar
¼ c. melted fat
1 c. sour cream
2½ c. flour
1 tsp. baking soda
½ tsp. salt
¼ c. cocoa

Add beaten egg to sugar and melted fat. Combine dry ingredients. Add dry ingredients and sour cream alternately to first mixture. Roll out, cut, and bake in moderate oven (375°F).

Variation:
Drop Cookies: Decrease the flour in the above recipe to 2 c. and drop dough by teaspoonfuls on greased sheet. Ice with chocolate powdered icing sugar: combine 1 c. sifted powdered sugar with 2 tbsp. unsweetened cocoa powder, ¼ tsp. vanilla, and 1 tbsp. milk in a bowl. Stir in additional milk, 1 tsp. at a time, until icing is thin enough to drizzle.

Good Cookies

October 1913

2 c. sugar, 1 c. butter, 1 c. sour cream or butter-milk, 3 eggs, 1 tsp. baking soda. Mix soft, roll thin, cut into shapes, sift granulated sugar over them and gently roll it in. Bake on buttered baking sheet in a hot oven (400°F).

Filled Cookies

March 1911

1 c. sugar, ½ c. shortening, 1 egg, ½ c. sweet milk, 1 tsp. flavoring extract of choice, 2 tsp. baking powder, ½ tsp. baking soda. Cream the sugar, shortening, and egg all together as for cake, add milk and flavoring. Have the flour sifted, work the soda and baking powder well through the dry flour to be used, then add the mixture. Make dough just hard enough to roll well. Roll very thin and cut with cookie cutters, place a layer of cookies in a greased pan, on each cookie put 1 tsp. jam, jelly, or preserves and place a cookie on top, press around the edges with a finger, pierce with a fork, and bake in a quick oven (400°F).

The Cookies That Went to Market
June 1928

2 eggs, well beaten
2 c. white sugar
1 c. lard (full)
1 c. sweet milk (scant)
⅓ tsp. nutmeg
1 tsp. vanilla
1 tsp. baking soda
1 tsp. baking powder

Mix and let stand overnight in refrigerator if possible as they will not need as much flour if you do.

Mix with pastry flour (editor's note: start with 1 c. and increase gradually, as necessary), as soft as you can easily handle on the board. If too stiff, add cream. Roll out on a floured board and cut with cookie cutters of your choice. Bake in hot oven with two raisins on top, also a sifting of white sugar.

Pack in large tin boxes that cookies and crackers are sold from in grocery stores. Sell at 20¢ a dozen.

Love Krandse (Danish)
March 1927

4 hard cooked egg yolks
1 c. butter
½ c. sugar, plus extra for dipping
3 c. flour
1 tsp. vanilla
1 egg, lightly beaten

Rub the egg yolks through a sieve. Cream the butter and sugar, and mix with the flour. Add the egg yolks, vanilla. Roll the dough thin and form in small wreaths. Dip in beaten egg and sugar. Place in pan and bake at 350°F.

—*Miss S.R., Nebraska*

❦ *Tea Spoon Savings* ❦

By E. Margaret Parker, May 1937

When I was first married, my husband's mother would frequently quote to me, "A woman can always throw out with a teaspoon more than a man can throw in with a shovel."

I don't think the adage really holds water. A woman would have to work much faster than most of us do to come anywhere near doing that with a man who was any kind of shoveller at all. But the idea evidently took root in me, for through the years since then I have accumulated a rather large-sized bag of little saving tricks which take care of those teaspoonfuls. However, I do not enjoy the saving so much now, as I do the products themselves, made from tidbits.

For example, aren't the rinds of oranges just too fresh and thick and golden to be thrown away? It seems as though there should be something to do with them. There is . . . the sweetened rind I use for orange bread, coffee cake or cookies. The fact that the rinds are an appreciable source of vitamin C does not, of course, lessen the home-maker's satisfaction in using them. The making does not require much more time or effort than to can the skins; and the process is practically the same:

Strips are cut . . . and these are boiled until tender. Then the juice is drained, and, to 4 orange peels, 2 c. sugar and 1 of water are added. The mixture is boiled until the strips appear transparent. Then they are lifted from the syrup, and, when slightly cooled, rolled in sugar. They should be dried on a flat dish or paper slightly, then stored in a covered container to keep fresh and tasty.

Orange Sugar Cookies

1 c. fat
1½ c. sugar
3 eggs
1 c. finely chopped candied orange peel (see above)
2 tsp. baking powder
½ tsp. salt
4 to 5 c. sifted flour
⅔ c. milk
1 tsp. lemon or orange extract

Cream fat, add sugar, eggs, orange peel, and then dry ingredients alternately with milk and extract. Roll and cut or shape in balls and flatten out. Bake in a moderately hot oven (400°F) for 10 minutes.

White Cookies
May 1932

1 c. butter
3 c. flour
2 eggs
1 c. sugar
3 tbsp. milk
1 tsp. baking soda
½ tsp. nutmeg

Mix butter and flour as for pie crust. Break eggs into dish and mix with sugar, milk, baking soda, and nutmeg. Combine with flour mixture. Roll out, cut, and bake at 350°F.

—*Mrs. M.M.V., Montana*

Scotch Short Bread
April 1923

3 c. flour
2 c. butter
1 c. sugar
1 oz. blanched almonds

Sift the flour twice and rub in the butter with the hands. Add the sugar and knead and mix either on a board or in a bowl until a dough is formed. Do not add either egg or milk, as the butter softens the mixing and will bind the ingredients together. Roll the dough rather thinly, cut into rounds or ovals, and press a few almonds onto each. Bake in a pie pan in a slow oven (300°F) until golden brown.

Refrigerator Cookies

Ice Box Cookies

1934

1 c. butter or part other fat
½ c. lard
1 c. granulated sugar
1 c. brown sugar, firmly packed
3 eggs
½ tsp. salt
1 tsp. cinnamon
½ tsp. baking soda
1 tsp. baking powder
1 c. nut meats
4½ c. flour

Cream the fats and sugars. Add the slightly beaten eggs and beat well. Sift the salt, cinnamon, baking soda, and baking powder with 1 c. flour; add to first mixture and beat well. Add the nut meats mixed with the rest of the flour. Mold into 2 well-shaped loaves and set in a cold place overnight. In the morning, slice and bake in a moderately hot oven (450°F).

Variations:
Use 1¾ c. white sugar and omit brown. Omit spice if desired

Divide dough into 2 parts and add sliced dates to 1 part and cocoanut to the other.

Butterscotch Cookies
December 1932

1½ c. butter
2 c. brown sugar
2 eggs
3 c. flour
2 tsp. baking powder

Cream butter, add sugar and well-beaten eggs. Mix well. Add flour and baking powder sifted together. Mix to a dough. Shape in rolls, wrap in waxed paper, and chill or store in cool place, a refrigerator if available. Slice thin, bake on buttered and floured cookie sheet in hot oven (400°F).

Chocolate Cookies
December 1930

½ c. shortening
1 c. sugar
1 egg
2 squares melted unsweetened chocolate
2 c. flour (measured before sifting)
¼ tsp. salt
2 tsp. baking powder
¼ c. milk

Cream the shortening, add the sugar and blend well. Add the well beaten egg and melted chocolate, and beat. Add the remaining dry ingredients and milk alternately. Chill dough and when firm, roll out and form in rolls the size of a tumbler (a cylinder of about 3 inches in length). Chill again until firm, then cut into thin slices. Bake on a greased pan or cookie sheet in moderate oven about 10 minutes. If dough is put in refrigerator, it may be kept several days wrapped in wax paper.

—A reader in Kansas

Mother Knows

OCCIDENT Flour is made from only the choicest portion of the finest wheat grown.

Every kernel in every bushel of that carefully selected wheat is washed and scoured before it goes through the long and thorough OCCIDENT Special milling processes.

Then there is unrelaxing vigilance at every stage of manufacture, including the baking of bread, to make absolutely certain that OCCIDENT Flour will fulfill our guarantee of better bread, or money back.

That is why OCCIDENT Flour is so wholesome and so nourishing and why so many women of long baking experience insist upon it.

Order this better flour for your next baking day. Make as many bakings as you wish and if you do not find OCCIDENT to be better than any other flour you have ever used return the unused portion of the sack and get your money back.

If you don't know your nearest OCCIDENT dealer write us.

**COSTS MORE
WORTH IT!**

RUSSELL-MILLER MILLING CO.   General Offices, Minneapolis, Minn.

SOMETHING TO THINK ABOUT

We operate 12 flour mills—two in Minneapolis, eight in North Dakota and two in Eastern Montana—with a combined daily capacity of 13,500 barrels flour and 500 tons wheat mill feed. Our wheat storage facilities are ample to permit of careful selection of the choicest hard wheats, insuring uniform flour quality over the entire year.

Wheat storage capacity—10 country mill elevators, 1,000,000 bushels; 3 terminal elevators, 8,750,000 bushels; 140 elevators situated in the heart of the hard wheat belt of North Dakota and Eastern Montana, 4,000,000 bushels—total combined capacity 13,750,000 bushels. These facilities for supplying the best hard wheat flour are unsurpassed.

OCCIDENT
The Guaranteed Flour

Holiday Cookies

Viennese Almond Cookies

December 1936

½ c. butter
1¾ cups sifted flour
½ c. sugar
½ c. finely ground, blanched almonds
2 egg yolks
2 to 2½ tbsp. cream

Work butter into flour until mealy (finer than for pie crust). Add sugar and nuts and mix well. Add beaten yolks, then cream. Dough should be soft enough to handle without breaking. For "horseshoes," roll in long strips about the thickness of a pencil. Cut in 3-inch lengths and shape each piece as a crescent or horseshoe. Bake in a moderately hot oven (400°F), about 15 minutes. While warm, roll in a mixture of sugar and ground nuts. Cover ends with a thin chocolate icing. (See recipe for Chocolate Glaze, page 99.)

Variation:

For jelly circles, roll dough quite thick, about ½ inch. Cut out very small rounds with a tiny cutter or wine glass. Make a dent in the center and put in a fleck of bright jelly. Sprinkle ground nuts and sugar around edge. Bake 10 to 15 minutes at 400°F.

Spritsbakelser (Swedish)

February 1928

1 c. butter
1 c. sugar
1 egg
2 tsp. almond extract
flour to make a stiff dough, from 2½ to 3 c.

Cream the butter and sugar, add the beaten egg, extract, and flour. Force through a cookie press to form into rings or fancy shapes. Bake in a hot oven (400°F), taking care not to burn.

—*Mrs. A.J., Iowa*

Sand Tarts

December 1930

½ c. butter
1½ c. brown sugar
2 eggs
3½ c. flour
½ tsp. cinnamon
2 tsp. baking powder
¼ c. granulated sugar mixed with ¼ tsp. cinnamon

Cream butter and sugar, add the beaten eggs, and sift in dry ingredients. Roll ½ inch thick, and sprinkle with cinnamon sugar. Cut out and bake quickly. Citron, raisins, orange peel, nuts or maraschino cherries make good decorations for these if wished.

—*A reader in Ohio*

❧ Old Country Christmas Cakes ❧

By Sarah Gibbs Campbell, December 1928

It was an old world custom for friends and neighbors to exchange Christmas cakes and many of their descendants in America still cling to this delightful tradition and also hand down the original recipes from generation to generation. These little cakes taste wonderfully good with either tea or coffee throughout the winter, but to be truly Christmas cakes, they must be cut in many shapes, some graceful and appropriate, others grotesque and quaint—moons and stars, horses, dogs, sheep, and quaint little figures of boys and girls. These recipes given will supply a delightful variety and if the quantities seem too large, it is quite easy to make only a half or a quarter of the amount, but before doing this, remember how long they will keep and what charming last-minute gifts or remembrances they will make.

Honey Cakes (German Christmas Cookies)

1 lb. sugar
1 lb. honey
1 tsp. baking soda dissolved in 2 tbsp. water
1 lb. flour
¼ tsp. cloves
¼ c. water
1 tsp. cinnamon
ground cardamom seed from 3 pods
juice and grated rind of 1 lemon
1 lb. pecan meats
¼ lb. ground citron

Put the sugar and honey in a saucepan, heat until the sugar is dissolved and the boiling point is reached. Remove from the fire and pour the mixture into a large bowl. Add the baking soda, dissolved in the water, immediately. Then stir in the flour and spices which have been sifted together, and the lemon juice and rind. Add the nuts and citron (all chopped fine), mix well, roll very thin, and cut. If dough is allowed to cool before rolling, the process will be very difficult. Allow cakes to stand, covered, overnight before baking. Bake at 350°F.

Dutch Christmas Cakes

1 c. butter
1 c. sugar
1 tsp. grated orange rind
6 tbsp. orange juice
4 or 5 c. flour

Cream the butter and sugar, stir in the orange rind and juice, then work in the sifted flour. The dough should be very stiff, so it is necessary to work in the last flour with the fingers. Chill and roll very thin, cut and sprinkle each cookie with pulverized sugar and cinnamon. For sprinkling, sift together 2 tbsp. sugar and 1 tsp. cinnamon. Sprinkle the tops of some of the cookies with grated, dried orange rind and granulated sugar. Bake at 350°F.

42

Molasses Cookies

½ c. lard
1¼ lbs. sugar
1 c. molasses
4 eggs
flour
¾ of a grated nutmeg
1 tsp. cinnamon
1 tsp. ground cloves
1 tsp. mace
1 tsp. baking powder
¼ tsp. baking soda
1 qt. pecan meats

Cream the lard and sugar, add molasses and slightly beaten eggs. Then sift 2 c. of flour with the spices, baking powder, and soda. Add to the first mixture, stir in the chopped pecans and enough flour to roll easily. Cut and bake in a moderate oven (350°F) for these cakes burn easily. This recipe is also from an old German cookbook.

Gingernuts (Old English)

½ c. butter
2 c. sugar
2 eggs
4 c. flour
2 tsp. ground ginger
1 tsp. each of cinnamon and ground cloves
½ c. chopped nuts
sugar for rolling
citron pieces or walnut halves for garnish

Cream the butter and sugar, beat in the eggs, then the flour sifted with the spices. The dough will seem quite stiff. Shape into little balls with the fingers, roll them in granulated sugar and press a piece of citron or half an English walnut into each and bake in a moderate oven (350°F).

German Springerle

February 1928

7 eggs
3 c. powdered sugar
1 tsp. grated nutmeg
1 tsp. cinnamon
1 tsp. vanilla
1 square unsweetened chocolate, grated
2 tbsp. butter
1 tsp. baking powder
1 c. flour

Separate whites and yolks of eggs, beat yolks and sugar, spices, vanilla, chocolate, and butter, which has been slightly softened to facilitate mixing. Fold in beaten egg whites. Mix baking powder with ½ the flour and stir or knead into mixture. Turn onto well floured board and knead in as much flour as dough will hold. Roll very thin and mold over single springerle mold or mold of any kind. Press dough on mold to make design distinct. Cut cakes out, lay on the table. Cover with clean cloth and let dry until morning. Bake in moderate oven (350°F) for about 20 minutes.

—*Mrs. A.W., Illinois*

44

Ginger Spice Cookies

1934

The crispy Christmas kind.

½ c. solid fat
½ c. molasses
½ c. milk
4 c. sifted flour
½ tsp. salt
1 tsp. baking soda
1 tsp. baking power
1 tsp. mixed spice ★
1 tsp. ground ginger
1 egg
1 c. sugar

Heat fat and molasses in saucepan until fat is melted. Add milk, beat well, pour into mixing bowl and set aside to cool. Sift flour, salt, baking soda, baking powder, and spices together. Beat egg; add sugar; add to molasses. Stir flour in gradually to form a smooth dough. Cover the dough and let ripen an hour on the counter. The dough is like putty—little flour is needed for rolling. Roll out to ⅛ inch thickness. Cut in rounds, oblongs, or fancy shapes. Bake on slightly greased pans in very moderate oven (350°F) until a light brown color.

★ Mixed spice, or pudding spice, is mixture commonly used in English cookery containing cinnamon, nutmeg, allspice, and often mace, cloves, ginger, coriander, and caraway. To make your own for the purposes of this recipe: mix together 1 tsp. allpsice, 1" stick cinnamon, ground, 1 tsp. cloves, ground, 1 tsp. grated nutmeg, and 1 tsp. ground ginger.

Drop Cakes for Holiday Baskets

December 1922

1 c. sugar (brown or white)
½ c. butter
2 eggs
½ c. sour cream
½ c. corn syrup
1 tsp. each cinnamon and ground cloves
1 tsp. baking soda
1 c. chopped raisins
1 c. chopped figs or dates
2½ c. flour
½ tsp. baking powder
½ c. black walnuts

Cream the sugar and butter, add eggs, then sour cream and syrup. Next add the spices and soda dissolved in 2 tbsp. hot water. Mix fruit with ½ c. flour to keep from settling. Add remaining flour and baking powder to the batter until stiff enough to drop, then stir in fruit and nuts and drop on greased pan. Bake at 350°F until golden brown. This makes about 3 dozen cookies.

To pack: Wrap each cookie in a square of oiled paper and fill a low sandwich basket. Place a spray of pine needles or holly across the top and tie a crisp bow of red tarletan on the handle. A large piece of white tissue paper, caught together with a sprig of green, covers the basket, cookies and all. This wrapping is suitable if the gift is to be delivered by hand. For the cookies which must be sent by parcel post, a white box is better. Each cookie is wrapped in oiled paper and a sprig of holly or pine needles is placed across the top of the box before the lid is put on. Wrap the box with white tissue paper, tie with red ribbon and slip in a pretty Christmas card.

Bars and Cake Squares

Filled Date Cookies

December 1934

Crumb mixture or streusel:
1½ c. flour
½ tsp. baking soda
½ tsp. salt
1 c. brown sugar
1½ c. rolled oats
1 c. melted butter
1 c. chopped nuts

Filling:
40 dates, chopped
1 c. water
1 c. sugar
½ tsp. vanilla

Cook filling in a saucepan over medium heat until thick and smooth, add vanilla, then cool.

To prepare crumb mixture, sift together flour, baking soda, and salt, and mix in sugar and oats. Add melted butter and nuts and mix thoroughly with the hands. Pat ½ of crumb mixture in a fairly shallow greased tin (9 x 13). Put date filling on top and then add remaining crumb mixture, patting down well. Bake at 350°F for 45 minutes. Cool, cut in strips or squares.

Raisin-and-Date Bars

November 1921

1 c. sugar
1 egg
1 tsp. vanilla
½ c. chopped raisins
½ c. seeded and chopped dates
½ c. chopped nuts
1 c. flour
2 tsp. baking powder
¼ tsp. salt

Mix the sugar, egg, and vanilla. Mix the fruit, nuts, and dry ingredients and add to the first mixture. Turn into an oiled tin (9 x 13) and bake in a moderate oven (350°F) for 30 minutes. Remove from the pan and when cool cut into narrow strips about 1 inch wide and 4 inches long. Roll each strip in powdered sugar and put away in a tin box.

Honey Fruit Cookies

July 1933

½ c. shortening
1 c. brown sugar
1 egg
½ c. honey
2½ c. flour
1 tsp. baking soda
½ tsp. salt
1 tsp. cinnamon
¼ tsp. allspice
¼ tsp. ground cloves
½ c. buttermilk
¼ c. raisins tossed in 1 tbsp. flour
1 c. chopped nuts
¼ c. shredded coconut

Cream shortening and sugar together, add egg well beaten, and honey. Add flour, sifted with baking soda, salt, and spices, alternately with buttermilk, then floured raisins, chopped nuts, and coconut. Mix all together well and spread thinly in well-greased shallow pans (9 x 13). Bake at 375°F for about 20 minutes. While still warm, spread thinly with icing made by moistening confectioner's sugar with milk or water and flavoring with vanilla. When cold, cut with knife in squares or diamonds and remove from the pan.

—*B.N., Nebraska*

48

Frosted Nut Cookies

January 1932

½ c. shortening
1 c. sugar
2 eggs, well beaten
½ tsp. vanilla
1½ c. flour, sifted before measuring
½ tsp. salt
1 tsp. baking powder
1 c. chopped nuts

Cream shortening, add sugar, and mix together well. Add eggs, vanilla, and flour with salt and baking powder. Spread ¼ inch thick on buttered baking sheet. Sprinkle with chopped nuts and cover with the following frosting:

Beat white of 1 egg, fold in 1 c. brown sugar, add ½ tsp. vanilla.

Bake at 375°F for 20 minutes. Cut in squares before entirely cool.

Cheese Torte

October 1933

1½ lbs. cottage cheese
8 egg yolks
3 tbsp. flour
1½ c. sugar
1½ c. cream
⅛ tsp. salt
grated rind and juice of 1 lemon
1½ tbsp. butter, well-creamed
8 egg whites, beaten until stiff

Mix in order given, folding in egg whites last. Bake in greased baking pan (9 x 13) dusted with fine breadcrumbs for ¾ hour in a moderate oven (350°F). Serve in squares.

Date Torte

February 1938

4 eggs, separated
¾ c. sugar
¾ c. flour
½ tsp. baking powder
pinch salt
½ lb. dates, cut
1 c. chopped walnuts

Method: Beat egg yolks and add sugar. Sift flour, baking powder, and salt. Add dates and nuts to the flour, rubbing well into the flour. Add the egg and sugar mixture, fold in beaten egg whites. Pour in well-greased shallow pan (9 x 13), bake in a slow oven (325°F) for 30 to 40 minutes. Serve in squares with whipped or ice cream.

Chocolate-Nut Sticks

January 1910

First mix carefully together 1 c. fine granulated sugar, ¼ c. melted butter, 1 unbeaten egg, 2 squares unsweetened chocolate (melted), ¾ tsp. vanilla, ½ c. flour, ½ c. English walnut meats cut in pieces. Line a 7-inch square pan with greased paper and spread mixture evenly in pan. Bake in a slow oven (275°F). As soon as removed from oven, cut cake in strips, using a long sharp knife. If these directions are not followed, the paper will cling to the cake and it will be impossible to cut in shapely pieces.

—*Woman's Home Companion for December*

Cakes

❧ *Table Talk* ❧
The Secret of Making Many Kinds of Cake Is Easily Learned

By Anna Barrows, September 1916

There are cakes and cakes, big and little, loaf and layer, of many colors, flavors and frostings, yet in all the many receipts there are just two types of cakes, the sponge cake and the butter cake.

In modern cook books we sometimes find the old-fashioned directions for sponge cake: "The weight of the eggs in sugar and half the weight of the eggs in flour." Sugar is about twice as heavy as flour so that according to the modern way of measuring, the formula would be: equal measures of sugar, egg and flour. To these proportions, with slight variation, we may reduce most cake receipts. Eggs vary much in size so that it may take only three or even as many as six eggs to fill a cup. Many receipts give these proportions: Four or five eggs, one cup of sugar, one cup of flour; a little salt and lemon juice and grated rind are commonly added.

The original sponge cakes were made before baking powder was invented. Now we try to make more cake with the number of eggs, or a cake of the same size with fewer eggs, so we often see receipts where water is added and more flour and the cake raised by one or two teaspoonfuls of baking powder.

An angel cake is a white sponge cake in which only the egg white is used and about eight egg whites are needed to fill a cup. Sometimes a little larger proportion of sugar is used in this cake.

The sunshine cakes have more egg whites than yolks but the total amount would be about the same.

Such cakes as these may be baked in one loaf, long, round or square, or in layer cakes or small shapes. The smaller they are the quicker they will heat and cook thru and hence the hotter the oven may be. Perhaps this is the reason we are more likely to bake small cakes and layer cakes in the gas and kerosene ovens, which are difficult to adjust to the lower temperature needed for layer and richer cakes.

Eggs cook at low temperature and if a crust is formed too soon on the surface of the cake, the air bubbles beneath, when they are expanded by the heat, cannot lift the crust and the cake is rather tough and not as light as it should be. Sometimes there is a softer place in the crust which gives way to the pressure of hot air beneath and the cake cracks irregularly on top. About three hundred degrees Fahrenheit is the right temperature when cake is put into the oven. The heat should increase gradually until the middle period of the time and then gradually decrease.

A large sponge cake should be put in a moderate oven which becomes a little hotter and then cooler toward the last.

When the cake is all in one loaf the oven should be of such a degree of heat that it may bake nearly an hour and still be a golden brown.

When we make cake, we should look to the oven heat first of all, remembering that it must not be too great. Next, measure the materials, prepare the grated lemon rind and put the juice over it.

To mix the cake: Separate the yolks and whites of the four or five eggs, putting yolks in the mixing bowl. Beat the yolks till they become lighter colored and thicken slightly; add the one cup of sugar, mix and let stand while beating the whites. If we have two beaters, we use the wheel beater for the yolks and the whisk to beat the whites on a flat dish or platter. If not, we must wash the beater with which we have beaten the yolks, for the oily nature of the yolks might interfere with the stiffening of the whites; or beat whites first and transfer the beater directly to the yolks. I prefer the first method. Strain the lemon juice from the rind into the yolks and sugar and mix. Then fold a portion of the stiff whites into the yolks and sugar, sift in part of the flour, add more whites and flour alternately till all is smoothly blended without stirring, but by cutting and wrapping the yolk over the white. Beating or stirring lets out the air we have beaten into the whites and makes the mixture more liquid. The cake when ready for the pans should be like whipped cream.

If put in small tins or layer-cake pans, such cake should bake twenty minutes or more. When taken from the oven too soon it shrinks too much. Better leave it in the oven a few minutes longer with the door ajar if necessary.

The butter cakes are mainly variations from the pound cake which was used generally in the days when housekeepers thought they must have cake always on hand. A cake made light with eggs only and with no other moisture than the eggs and butter did not dry like a modern cake containing milk or water and baking powder.

The proportions fit most simple cakes are, in general: one measure fat, two measures sugar, one measure liquid, one measure eggs, four or more measures of flour, with one teaspoonful of baking powder to each cup of flour.

The time-honored way of mixing such cakes is to cream the butter or other fat. That is to work and beat it until like cream, by this means mixing in some air as when whipping cream or beating eggs. This is an easy process if hot water is put in the clean bowl and left there while measuring the ingredients for the mixture. Then wipe out the bowl, put in the butter, cut in slices and leave in a few moments, perhaps while greasing the pans. By that time the butter will have softened a little and when rubbed against the bowl with a wooden spoon, quickly is beaten light.

Why not use one receipt on which you can rely as the basis for a variety of cakes?

Sponge Cakes

Yolk Sponge Cake
October 1932

6 to 7 egg yolks (for ½ c.)
½ c. water
1 tbsp. lemon juice
½ tsp. grated lemon rind
1 c. sugar
1½ c. cake flour
2 tsp. baking powder
¼ tsp. salt

Beat egg yolks until thick and lemon colored (3 minutes).
Add water and beat for 2 minutes. Add lemon juice and rind.
Beat sugar gradually into egg yolks, until light and thoroughly blended.
Fold sifted dry ingredients gradually into egg and sugar mixture.
Bake in an ungreased medium-size tube pan in a moderate oven (350°F), about 45 to 50 minutes. Invert pan and cool before removing.

Hot Water Sponge Cake
March 1916

2 eggs, separated
¾ c. sugar
6 tbsp. hot water
½ tbsp. lemon juice
1 c. flour
1½ tsp. baking powder
¼ tsp. salt

Beat yolks of eggs until thick; add half the sugar, then the water, lemon juice, and remaining sugar; fold in the stiffly-beaten whites of the eggs and the flour which has been mixed and sifted with the baking powder and the salt. Bake in a greased cake pan at 350°F for 20 to 30 minutes.

When You Make A Cake
Does It Fairly Melt In Their Mouths?

ANNA COYLE

THAT knack of making really wonderful cakes may so easily be acquired. Perfect assurance of success comes when you use a reliable foundation recipe and select just the right ingredients. Fluffy white cakes with creamy fudge frosting, delicious dark ones rich with dates and nuts, or raisins and crystallized fruit, angel food cakes as light as a feather, are only a few of the tempting varieties made from a plain white cake or sponge cake recipe.

For cake of excellent quality select only the choicest materials and have at hand the best possible equipment for mixing and baking. Plan every step in order, measure all ingredients accurately and have everything ready before beginning to mix the cake. Oven temperature is very important. Cakes in oven must be handled carefully.

What could bring more birthday joy to young or old than a perfect angel food cake, beautifully iced and decorated with a candle for each year or the conventional dozen candles? Small iced cakes are for special occasions and are appropriate served for refreshments with ice cream. Chocolate, tutti-frutti and coconut cakes are always popular.

Bridecake calls for your very best white cake and white frosting. Almond is its distinguishing flavor. Fruit cake is for the groom. Tiny white boxes are filled with white and dark cake, tied with white ribbon and presented to guests. The girls will tuck these under their pillows to dream on. These boxes usually replace the groom's cake.

Plain White Cake: Cream ½ cup of butter with wooden spoon and gradually add 1 cup fine granulated sugar to butter, beating mixture between each addition.

Sift together 2 cups flour and 3 teaspoons baking powder.

Beat 4 egg whites until light but not dry, using a wire egg beater.

Measure ⅔ cup milk and add to butter mixture alternately with flour and baking powder. Beat the entire mixture until smooth, then fold in the beaten egg whites. This is done with a wooden spoon to mix eggs evenly through cake mixture and not break down the air cells.

Butter cake pan and dust with flour. Spread batter evenly in pan, which should be two-thirds full if cake is to rise to fill pans. Bake 35 minutes in moderately hot oven for first 10 minutes, then increase heat until three-fourths of baking time and gradually reduce heat. Test with clean straw. Cake shrinks from edge of pan when done. Turn out of pans at once on cake or bread rack covered with tea towel.

A day each week for cake making, called "cake day" is quite as important in the well-ordered household as wash day and cleaning day. Cake is a real food and the cake box should never be empty.

It is frequently an economy of time and gives pleasing variety to make two cakes at one time, using the same batter in the layers of both cakes with different icings.

A thermometer simplifies making icings.

Additional recipes will be found on another page in this magazine. Try these in your home baking and when making a cake for the neighborhood gathering, the church supper or to sell. Many women and girls have found homemade cakes a satisfactory source of income.

Sponge Cake: 5 eggs, 1 cup fine granulated sugar, 1 cup flour (well sifted), 1 tablespoon lemon juice, 1 tablespoon cold water, ¼ teaspoon salt.

Beat yolks until thick and lemon colored. Add sugar gradually and continue beating with Dover beater. Add lemon juice and water. Cut and fold in beaten egg whites. When whites are partly folded in, gradually begin adding flour (mixed with salt). Cut and fold in lightly. Do not beat. Bake 40 to 60 minutes in slow oven. Test with straw.

Sponge Cake Pudding
June 1934

Bake a sponge cake (see previous recipes) in a flat-bottomed pudding dish; when ready to use, cut in 6 or 8 pieces, split and spread with butter and return to the dish. Make an uncooked custard of 4 eggs, 1 qt. milk, 1 tsp. vanilla, and sweeten to taste (editor's note: ¼ c. sugar is about right). Pour over the cake and bake at 350°F for about ½ hour. The cake will swell and fill with custard.

—*Mrs. A.W., California*

The Farmer's Wife *food editor's note: I used some left-over sponge cake, cut to fit a glass baking dish, this must be baked in a moderate, not hot oven. A sauce made of tart fruit as rhubarb or lemon is good with this.*

Mrs. Laird's Coveted Nut-Caramel Cake
June 1928

Start with 2 eggs, well beaten until light-colored. Add 1 tsp. vanilla and 1 c. white sugar. Beat well again.

Take 1 c. pastry flour into which 1 heaping tsp. of baking powder has been thoroughly sifted. Sift into batter and cut it in, as you would pastry. Then add ½ c. boiling water and beat well again. Bake in 2 large layers. Ice with Boiled Icing III (see page 101). Decorate the top with halves of nut meats.

Sell for home trade at 75¢ each; for market at $1.00 each.

Orange Sunshine Cake with Whipped Cream Topping

February 1936

5 eggs, separated
1½ c. sugar
½ c. orange juice
1½ c. cake flour
¼ tsp. salt
½ tsp. baking powder
¾ tsp. cream of tartar

Beat yolks until thick and light, adding half of the sugar. Add orange juice and beat. Sift flour, salt, and baking powder together three times and add. Beat whites until foamy, add cream of tartar, then rest of sugar gradually. Fold into other mixture. Bake in an ungreased tube pan in a very slow oven (325°F) for 1 hour. Cool, remove from pan, and ice with whipped cream, very slightly sweetened. Sprinkle with grated orange rind.

—*L.H., Colorado*

Kiss Cake

June 1936

3 large egg whites
dash salt
few drops lemon juice or vinegar
1 c. finely granulated sugar
1½ c. powdered sugar
whipped cream
strawberries

The success of meringues depends upon thorough beating of sugar into egg whites and slow baking. Whites whip up best at room temperature. Beat until stiff and dry, adding salt. Add vinegar or lemon, then add sugar gradually, beating after each addition. When finished, the meringue will be very stiff and satiny in appearance. Cover a greased baking sheet with parchment paper. Shape meringues into 3 round, flat layers, making them graduated in size with the largest one about 9 inches across. Bake in a very slow oven (250°F to 275°F) for 45 minutes. They will be a very pale brown. Pile whipped cream and strawberries between layers, and whipped cream over the top.

The Cake That Phoebe Jane Baked

Another Champion Visits the Country Kitchen

By Miriam J. Williams, April 1937

This is a house-that-Jack-built kind of story because the events which led to Phoebe Jane Huff's coming to the Country Kitchen to bake angel food cake unfold on paper like a nursery rhyme. But this story runs back aways in time. It begins with a 14-year-old club girl's wish to do her part, and keeps on to a 20-year-old college junior's thrill in a trip to St. Paul.

It was all because a 4-H Club leader near Leesburg, Ohio, asked one of her girls if she would exhibit an angel food cake at the country fair. When Mrs. Allen left instructions with this inexperienced four-teen-year-old club member, she knew that it would take some practicing at home to make a successful cake. But since Phoebe Jane was in foods club work to learn, she and her mother immediately went into conference. Mrs. Huff answered her daughter's questions as best she could and then suggested that she consult a neighbor who had a rep-utation for angel food. In Phoebe Jane's own words, "Mrs. Moore laughed when I told her what the club leader had asked me to do. Right that afternoon she took me to her kitchen and there my cake career began, when she began telling me many things about angel foods that I should remember.

"The first afternoon I did not do a thing but watch. The second afternoon I was allowed to measure some of the ingredients and do part of the mixing. On the last afternoon I mixed the cake and regu-lated the oven by myself."

The exhibition at the country fair was a success. Then later, in high school, an enterprising young brother suggested that Sis advertise in the school paper, of which he was business manager. Surprisingly enough, the orders which came in a few weeks also took care of all the extra Huff eggs. In that school year, 120 cakes were sold, almost entirely by favorable comment where these cakes were served.

Phoebe Jane's Angel Food Cake

1 c. sifted cake flour
1½ c. sugar
1¼ c. egg whites
½ tsp. salt
1 tsp. cream of tartar
2 tbsp. water
1 tsp. vanilla

Sift flour once before measuring, then sift 4 times with ½ c. of the sugar. Beat egg whites with a rotary beater, adding salt, cream of tartar, water, and vanilla when they are foamy. Beat whites just until they peak, and are still moist and shiny. With flat beater or mixing spoon, fold in remaining sugar, sifting one or two tbsp. at a time over surface and gently folding it in (about 50 strokes). Fold sifted flour and sugar mixture in the same way (about 90 strokes). Pour into ungreased angel food cake pans, and bake immediately in slow oven (325°F) for 1 hour or until surface of cake, when pressed lightly with finger, springs back into place. It should be at its full height and have a delicate brown color, and be shrunken slightly from the pan. Let cool in the inverted pan an hour before removing.

This is the foam, shiny and light, made by the beater, sturdy and bright, that beat the whites, a cup and a quarter, with measures of salt and cream of tartar

This is the sugar, a cup is right, cut into the foam, shiny and light, made by the beater, sturdy and bright

This is the flour with its share of sugar, sifted four times to make it bigger, folded so neat, into egg whites, flavored and sweet

This is the batter, light as foam, scrap from the bowl's shining dome, into pan especially planned for the angel fo cake that Phoebe Jane baked

Sponge Cake Roll

August 1936

3 eggs
1 c. sugar
1 tbsp. milk
1 c. pastry flour
1 tsp. baking powder
¼ tsp. salt

Beat eggs until light, add sugar gradually and continue beating. Stir in milk and then add the flour, which has been sifted with baking powder and salt. Line a shallow pan about 10x15 inches with greased parchment or wax paper, pour in batter evenly and bake in a moderately hot oven (375°F) for 12 minutes. Turn out on waxed paper sprinkled with powdered sugar. Remove the paper from bottom of cake. Cut off a thin strip as far as the crust extends on side of cake. Spread caramel filling (below) on cake, which is still slightly warm and roll. Wrap in slightly dampened towel and allow to cool. Serve each slice topped with a spoonful of soft vanilla ice cream. Makes 8 generous servings.

Caramel Filling:
1 c. sugar
1¼ c. boiling water
1/3 c. flour
1 c. milk
1 tbsp. butter
1 tsp. vanilla

Caramelize ½ c. sugar by slowly melting it in a saucepan. Add water and cook until the caramel has dissolved. In a double boiler, combine the remainder of the sugar with the flour and mix to a smooth paste with the milk. Add caramel syrup to this and cook over hot water stirring constantly until thick and smooth. Add butter and vanilla. Cool.

Lemon Roll

(8 Servings)

March 1936

Cake:
6 eggs, separated
½ c. sugar
1 tbsp. lemon juice
1 tsp. grated lemon rind
½ c. cake flour
½ tsp. baking powder
¼ tsp. salt
½ pt. heavy cream, whipped

Beat egg whites, adding sugar gradually until stiff and smooth. Beat yolks, add lemon juice and rind and fold into whites. Sift flour, baking powder, and salt 2 or 3 times and fold into egg mixture. Line a 10x15-inch pan with waxed paper, which has been greased, and spread in sponge mixture. Start in a very slow oven, bringing up to 250°F. Bake just until firm but not brown. If a regulated oven, bake until cake is raised, then turn off heat and let cake stay in oven until firm. Turn onto a clean towel, sprinkled liberally with powdered sugar and remove waxed paper. Let stand about 30 minutes until cool, then roll cake up in cloth like a jelly roll, rolling it the long way of the cake. Let stand 10 minutes. Unroll, spread with part of whipped cream (unsweetened) and roll up. Sprinkle roll with powdered sugar, wrap in waxed paper and store in cool place until used.

Sauce:
1 c. sugar
grated rind and juice of 1 lemon
3 tbsp. cornstarch
⅔ c. water
1 egg or 2 yolks, beaten
½ tbsp. butter

Mix sugar, lemon rind, and cornstarch, add water and cook 10 minutes in double boiler, stirring until thickened. Add eggs and butter. Add lemon juice and cool. To serve, slice roll. Top each piece with a spoonful of whipped cream and over that a spoonful of lemon sauce.

—Mrs. W.K., Minnesota

Chocolate Roll

1934

3 eggs, separated
3 tbsp. powdered sugar
3 tbsp. cocoa

Filling:
⅔ c. whipping cream
1 tbsp. powdered sugar
½ tsp. vanilla
chocolate sauce

Beat yolks and powdered sugar for 8 minutes, add the cocoa. Turn into shallow pan (8x8 inch) lined with waxed paper. Bake 15 to 20 minutes in a moderately hot oven (375°F to 400°F). Turn out on damp cloth. Cool until barely warm, spread with whipped and flavored cream. Roll and place in ice box until serving. Slice and serve with a spoonful of whipped cream topped with chocolate sauce (such as Chocolate Glaze, page 99).

Maple Torte

July 1918

2 eggs, separated
½ c. maple sugar
¼ c. cornstarch
2 tbsp. barley flour
¼ tsp. baking powder
¼ tsp. salt

Beat the yolks of the eggs until light, add the sugar and beat until all is dissolved. Beat the whites until very stiff and fold into the yolks. Mix and sift the remaining ingredients several times and very gently and gradually fold into the egg mixture. Pour into a greased pan and bake in a very slow oven (275°F to 300°F) about 35 minutes. Serve with whipped cream.

Butter Cakes

Lazy Daisy Cake

May 1934

A delicious, light emergency cake

½ c. milk
1 tbsp. butter
2 eggs
1 c. sugar
1 c. sifted flour
1 tsp. baking powder
pinch of salt
1 tsp. vanilla

Put milk and butter in a saucepan on to heat. Beat eggs, add sugar, beat all together. Stir in dry ingredients sifted together once and vanilla. Then add hot milk, stirring carefully as it is added. Pour into flat greased pan and bake 25 to 30 minutes in a moderate oven (350°F to 375°F). While the cake is baking, stir up the topping.

Topping:
⅔ c. brown sugar
⅓ c. melted butter
4 tbsp. cream
½ c. coconut

Spread on warm cake and put under broiler for 5 to 10 minutes until frosting caramelizes. Instead of cocoanut, shredded blanched almonds or peanuts may be used on top and toasted with the icing.

Without a broiler, make the topping with only 2 tbsp. cream and spread on top while the cake is warm. Return to oven in the hottest place and leave until the icing caramelizes somewhat, but not long enough to dry out the cake.

64

Lady Baltimore Cake

October 1923

½ lb. butter
1 lb. sugar
½ pint milk
1 lb. flour
2 tsp. baking powder
2 tsp. almond extract
8 egg whites

Cream butter and sugar, add milk very slowly with flour and baking powder to keep smooth, then extract and finally the whites beat very light and bake in 2 layer cake pans (375°F) for 30 minutes.

Filling:
¾ c. boiling water
3 c. sugar
whites of 4 eggs
½ tsp. cream of tartar
1 tsp. vanilla
2 c. English walnuts, chopped
2 c. raisins, chopped

Pour boiling water on sugar and boil for 10 minutes until it ropes from the spoon. Have whites of eggs well beaten, add cream of tartar. Pour hot syrup over the whites while beating. Season with vanilla. Add walnuts and raisins to half this mixture, which you will use between layers of the cake; use the remaining icing to glaze the top and sides of the cake.

little butterfly gets her man

SWANS DOWN
CAKE FLOUR
A GENERAL FOODS PRODUCT

Virginia Silver Cake

December 1913

¾ lb. butter, 2 c. white sugar (loaf sugar pounded and sifted is the best here), 1½ c. flour, ½ c. cornstarch, 1 tsp. cream of tartar, whites of 18 eggs. Cream the butter with the sugar then sift the flour, cornstarch, and cream of tartar gradually into the butter; add last of all the beaten whites; flavor with 1 tsp. almond extract. Turn out into a greased cake pan. This cake requires much watching in baking and a slow oven (275°F).

White Cake with Cherry Frosting

February 1936

½ c. butter or part other fat
1 c. sugar
3 egg whites, unbeaten
1 tsp. vanilla
2 c. cake flour
3 tsp. baking powder
¼ tsp. salt
⅔ c. milk

Cream shortening, add sugar slowly, beating until fluffy. Add unbeaten whites, one at a time, beating very thoroughly after each addition, then add vanilla. Sift together dry ingredients, add alternately with milk to first mixture. Make into a large loaf or two layers. Bake in a moderate oven (375°F). A slightly less moist but lighter cake results if whites are folded in last.

Frost with Cherry Frosting (page 106).

Whipped Cream Cake with Boiled Marshmallow Icing

February 1939

1 c. heavy cream
2 eggs
1 c. sugar
1 tsp. vanilla
1½ c. sifted cake flour
2 tsp. baking powder
½ tsp. salt

Whip cream until stiff. Drop in unbeaten eggs, one at a time, and sugar, beating after each addition. (If eggs are large, one white may be omitted and used for a Seven-Minute Icing.) Add vanilla. Put dry ingredients into a sifter and fold lightly, blend well. Bake in a 9-inch square pan or 2 small layers or cupcakes for 25 to 30 minutes in a moderate oven (350°F to 375°F).

Let cool on rack, un-mold, and ice with Boiled Marshmallow Icing (page 101).

Variation:
Frost with Caramel Nut Icing (page 102).

Cocoanut Cake with Seven-Minute Icing

February 1936

⅓ c. butter or part other fat
1 c. sugar
1 whole egg and 2 yolks, unbeaten
2 c. cake flour
2 tsp. baking powder
¼ tsp. salt
¾ c. milk
¼ tsp. lemon extract or ½ tsp. vanilla

Cream butter thoroughly, add sugar gradually and cream again. Add egg and yolks and beat until creamy and light. Add dry ingredients, sifted 3 times, alternately with milk. Flavor, beat until smooth. Bake in two 9-inch layers in moderate oven (350°F). Put layers together with Seven-Minute Icing (page 102) from 2 egg whites reserved, sprinkling each layer thickly with unsweetened grated cocoanut.

—Mrs. J.M., New York

Walnut Layer Cake
May 1912

Put 4 beaten eggs into a basin, add 6 oz. (¾ c.) sugar and a pinch of salt and beat until light. Add 2 oz. melted butter, 2 tbsp. chopped walnut meats, 1 tsp. baking powder, and flour to thicken. Beat very thoroughly and add 1 tsp. vanilla and bake in 2 layers in greased cake pans, at 350°F. For filling use peach or apricot marmalade to which has been added chopped nut meats and do not frost the top of the cake.

Dutch Cake
April 1929

1 c. brown sugar
2 c. flour (or a little less)
½ c. buttermilk
2 eggs
1 tsp. baking soda
1 tbsp. maple syrup

Topping:
1 c. brown sugar
½ c. butter

Combine by conventional method of cake mixing. After pouring batter into cake pan, mix the topping ingredients and drop by ½ teaspoonfuls on top of batter. Bake in a moderate oven (350°F). The sugar and butter will sink into the cake at different levels, making this an unusual dessert.

Nectar Raisin Cake with Coffee Butter Icing

February 1936

1 c. raisins
½ c. shortening
¾ c. sugar
1 egg, beaten
½ tsp. vanilla
1¾ c. all-purpose flour
1 tsp. each of cinnamon, allspice, and nutmeg
½ tsp. baking powder
½ tsp. salt
½ tsp. baking soda
1 c. nuts

Put raisins in 1 c. boiling water and cook 10 minutes. Drain, saving ¾ c. of this water for the cake. Cream shortening, add sugar, cream until fluffy. Add egg and vanilla and beat well. Sift all dry ingredients except the baking soda. Add baking soda to raisin water and add alternately with the flour mixture. Add nuts and raisins, which have been dredged with a little of the flour. Bake in a loaf or layers in a very moderate oven (350°F). Top with Coffee Butter Icing (page 99).

—*Mrs. C.W., California*

❧ Mrs. Lyons' Pineapple Cake ❧

May 1927

From the time the story of the baking success of Mrs. C.A. Lyons of West Virginia appeared in *The Farmer's Wife*, there has been a steady demand for the recipe for her wonderful pineapple cake. Hundreds of letters have poured in, like the following one from a woman in South Dakota:

> Dear Editors: Enclosed you will find a check for a subscription to *The Farmer's Wife*.
> I should like to get the recipe for the wonderful pineapple cake of Mrs. Lyons. It might help some of our women in South Dakota. Am I asking too much? I will try to repay you in some other way.

—Mrs. G.C.E,
South Dakota

Although it was in the nature of a trade secret which means money to Mrs. Lyons, we finally decided to ask if she would be willing to publish the recipe for the benefit of readers of *The Farmer's Wife*.

Mrs. Lyons with her usual graciousness, promptly consented and we are very happy to give it in full, with recipes for filling and icing and directions for baking.

"I am glad the pineapple cake recipe is to be published because, I am sorry to say, I have a few unanswered requests for it," says Mrs. Lyons in her letter. "I have been deluged with letters and am trying to answer them in turn.

In my baking, I use accurate measurements, good ingredients and the right temperature.

In baking cakes I always cream the butter well before adding sugar. I find it necessary to cream the butter. After once having the butter well creamed the mixture is easily kept nice and creamy until it is put in the pan for baking.

I do not tip-toe around the kitchen after the cake is placed in the oven because if the cake is made as it should be and the heat of the oven correct, walking about will not cause a cake to fall. I am careful, however, in moving a cake around in the oven before it is well set.

I am never too old to learn and am more than willing to try new things and new ways."

Pineapple Cake

Cream well 1 c. butter
Add 2 c. granulated sugar
Add alternately 1½ c. milk and 4 c. cake flour. Sift once and then measure flour and then add 6 level tsp. of baking powder and sift again. Beat batter hard after each addition of milk.
Last fold in stiffly beaten whites of 6 eggs.
Add flavoring—I like pineapple or lemon (editor's note: 2 tsp. of extract)
This bakes 2 large layers. Bake 1 hour to 1 hour and 15 minutes.
I bake in a moderate oven (350°F) and bake until done regardless of time.

Filling:
Boil 1 c. granulated sugar and 1 c. water until it forms a soft ball. Add 1 large can of pineapple, which has been drained and diced, and cook until it forms a thick syrup but be careful not to cook until pineapple turns dark. Remove and cool. When cake and filling are cold, put filling over both layers and cover each with Boiled Icing I (page 100). We like this cake not put together but finished separately. (Sell for $1.50 per layer).

Raspberry Cake

(2 layer)
December 1930

½ c. butter
1 c. granulated sugar
2 eggs
2 tbsp. buttermilk
1 tsp. baking soda
1 c. raspberries
2 c. flour
½ tsp. cream of tartar

Cream the butter, add the sugar and blend well. Add eggs, well beaten, and the buttermilk in which the baking soda has been mixed. Add raspberries and flour and cream of tartar, which have been sifted together. Use any Boiled Icing (page 100).

—*A reader from New York*

German Apple Cake

May 1927

2½ c. flour
pinch of salt
1 tsp. baking powder
2 tbsp. butter or lard
1 c. milk
6 tart apples
cinnamon, sugar, unsalted butter

Mix the first five ingredients into a dough, roll out to ½ inch thick. Line a square tin with dough to 1 inch from top. Pare and core and quarter apples to fill in, standing apples on ends. Sprinkle with sugar, cinnamon, and bits of butter. Bake and serve as any cake (350°F until cooked through.)

—*Mrs. E.I.K, North Dakota*

Lemon Layer Cake

February 1913

3 eggs
6 tbsp. sugar
grated rind of 1 lemon
6 tbsp. flour
1 tsp. baking powder
1½ oz. butter, melted

Put the eggs, sugar, and grated lemon rind into a basin, stand it over a pan of boiling water, and whisk until warm. Then remove and continue whisking until quite cold and stiff. Then add the flour mixed with the baking powder, and the melted butter, taking care to stir it very gently, but on no account to beat it. Pour into cake pans which have been buttered and floured, bake 10 minutes in a moderate oven (350°F). Before turning out, allow the pans to stand 2 or 3 minutes. When cold, spread each thickly over with lemon mixture (see below); lay the rounds together, divide into 12 pieces, dust with powdered sugar, and serve.

Lemon Mixture:
Put into a saucepan ¾ c. sugar, yolks of 4 eggs, white of 1 egg, grated rind and strained juice of 1 large lemon, and 2 oz. butter. Stir over a gentle heat until it thickens. Pour onto a plate, and when cool use.

Checker Board Cake

October 1913

Editor's note: The original recipe for this cake calls for square pans, with light and dark batter poured in, alternately, in strips, but this is a tricky and time-consuming maneuver; the farmer's wife either used dividers of her own making, or achieved deftness in the pouring, freehand, after years of practice. Contemporary bakers are advised to use round checkerboard cake pans, which can be purchased at most kitchen supply shops.

Light Part:
½ c. butter, 1¼ c. granulated sugar, ½ c. water or sweet milk, 1 tsp. vanilla, 2 c. sifted pastry flour, 1 rounding tsp. baking powder, whites of 4 eggs.

Cream butter and sugar, add water, vanilla, flour, and baking powder, then whites of eggs beaten stiff. Set aside.

Dark Part:
2 c. sifted pastry flour, 1 rounding tsp. baking powder, ½ c. butter, ½ c. sugar (brown or white), yolks of 4 eggs, well beaten, 1 square melted sweetened chocolate, ½ tsp. each ground cloves, nutmeg, and cinnamon, ½ c. water or milk.

Sift flour and measure, add baking powder and sift 3 times. Cream butter and sugar. Add yolks and beat hard, then chocolate, then flour, spices, and water.

Grease paper, then grease and flour the cake pans. Assemble divider rings and pour batter into each section, alternating light and dark; if you began with light on the outside of the first pan, begin with dark for the second. Bake until a tester comes out clean (approximately 20 to 25 minutes). Cool and remove cakes from pans. Then stack and cover with any good icing.

Fudge Cake

November 1937

½ c. fat
1¼ c. sugar
2 eggs or 3 yolks
2 squares melted unsweetened chocolate
1 c. milk
2 c. cake flour
2 tsp. baking powder
½ tsp. salt
1 tsp. vanilla

Cream fat, add sugar and cream until light and fluffy. Beat in eggs, add chocolate and then alternately add milk and sifted dry ingredients. Add vanilla and bake in 2 layers, or a rectangular pan for squares, or as cupcakes, in moderate oven (350°F). Ice with any creamy chocolate icing (such as Chocolate Butter Frosting, page 105).

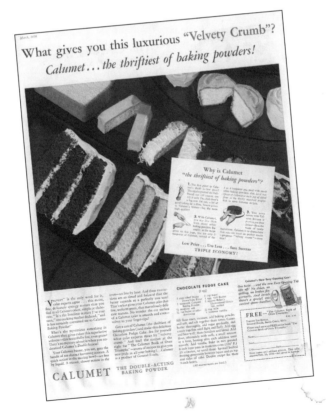

Big Bowl Cocoa Cake

November 1937

A large emergency cake, rich and moist.

1 c. cocoa
1 c. fat
1 tsp. baking soda
1 tbsp. cinnamon
1 c. boiling water
1 c. milk
1 tbsp. vanilla
2 eggs
1 tsp. salt
1 tsp. baking powder
2½ c. sugar
3 c. sifted flour
broken nut meats

In a big bowl put cocoa, fat, which may be sweet-flavored or clarified meat drippings, baking soda, and cinnamon. Pour over it the boiling water and stir until smooth. Add milk, vanilla, unbeaten eggs, and sift in the salt, baking powder, sugar, and flour which have been put into the sifter. Beat until smooth and free from lumps. Pour the batter, which is quite thin, into 2 greased square pans or a large rectangular dripping pan. Sprinkle top with nuts. Bake at once in very moderate (325°F) oven for about 40 minutes. (Needed: one big bowl, one big mixing spoon, a teaspoon, a sifter, one or two baking pans, and a very moderate oven.)

Raleigh Special Layer Cake

December 1925

Assemble following ingredients:

1 c. butter
2 c. sugar
4 eggs, separated
1 c. water
3 c. sifted flour
2 rounded tsp. baking powder

Prepare 4 layer cake pans, grease well, and dredge with flour. Cream butter thoroughly, gradually add 1 c. sugar and beat until fluffy. Beat egg yolks until very creamy then add second cup sugar gradually and beat well. Add this to first mixture and beat thoroughly. Begin adding water, just a little at a time—if possible add all the water before beginning to add the flour but if creamy mass begins to separate, then add a little flour and then remaining water. Fold in flour, a cupful at a time and continue in this folding until this is a smooth batter. Beat egg whites until stiff but not dry. Fold these into batter. Sift into this batter baking powder and beat this just a few minutes—to be sure baking powder is evenly distributed. Pour batter into pans. Bake in a quick oven (400°F) for 15 or 20 minutes.

Make Boiled Icing II (page 100) and add to it the following filling:

Ambrosia Filling:
½ c. crushed, drained pineapple
1 c. grated coconut
1 peeled orange, cut into pieces

Add to the boiled, cooled icing first the pineapple. Spread this on layers, add bits of orange and sprinkle coconut over this, add another layer, spread icing, dot with orange bits and sprinkle coconut on top. Build up your cake and cover top just as you did the layers.

"Lady Webb" Cake

December 1925

1 c. butter
2 c. sugar
4 c. flour
6 egg whites
1 c. water
2 heaping tsp. baking powder

Mix and bake in 3 layers at 350°F. For the filling use double the amount of Boiled Icing II (page 100) and add to this:

1 c. grated coconut
1 c. nut meats
1 c. chopped raisins
juice of 1 orange and 1 lemon

Spread between layers and on top. Add coconut sprinkled on top. An additional ¼ c. chopped raisins may be dredged in flour and added to batter for middle layer of 3-layer cake.

This is a lovely cake used. "I consider these my best Christmas cakes," says Mrs. Dixon.

❧ Interesting Facts about Food ❧

By Miriam J. Williams, February 1936

Recent studies in baking have shown that the freshness of cakes and special breads is preserved if they are baked in oven-proof glass and stored in the dish in which they were baked. Left-over rolls, nut breads, cornbread, gingerbread, even cake which has been covered and stored is reheated right in the container. The result is a pleasingly fresh taste, even three days or longer after the product was first baked.

Petit Fours

April 1931

⅓ c. fat
1½ c. sugar
3 c. pastry flour
1 tsp. salt
4 tsp. baking powder
1 c. milk
½ tsp. almond extract
3 egg whites

Cream fat, add sugar gradually, creaming continually. Add sifted dry ingredients alternating with milk and extract. Fold in stiffly beaten egg whites. Bake in flat square pans for about 30 minutes in medium oven (350°F); then cut in small squares with a very sharp knife. Ice with different colored icings (see Icing for Petit Fours, page 103).

Cherry Shortcake

June 1910

Sift together 2 c. flour, ¼ c. sugar, 4 level tsp. baking powder, a pinch of nutmeg, and a ½ tsp. salt. Rub in ⅓ c. butter, add 1 well-beaten egg and ⅔ c. sweet milk. Roll out in 2 thin cakes, butter the top of one, lay the other on it, and bake (350°F). When done, separate the layers, spread with butter, and put between and on top plenty of cherries, stoned, sweetened well, and mixed with thick sweet cream.

Gingerbread Banana Shortcake

June 1928

1¾ c. flour
1 tsp. ground ginger
½ tsp. cinnamon
½ tsp. salt
½ tsp. baking soda
3 tbsp. shortening
½ c. sugar
1 egg
½ c. molasses
½ c. boiling water

Sift dry ingredients together. Mix as for cake, bake in a pan where the dough will be about one inch thick. It will take from 25 to 30 minutes in a moderate (350°F) oven. While slightly warm, cover with sliced bananas and pile with whipped cream.

Rhubarb Shortcake

May 1931

3 eggs, separated
3 tbsp. lemon juice
1 c. sugar
1 c. flour
1 tsp. baking powder
¼ tsp. salt

Beat the yolks of the eggs until they are light. Add the lemon juice, and gradually beat in the sugar. Beat the whites of the eggs until they are dry, add them to the mixture and beat it well. Sift together the flour, baking powder, and salt. Fold the dry ingredients lightly into the egg mixture. Bake the cake in 2 layers in a moderate oven (350°F).

Filling:
2 tsp. gelatin
¼ c. cold water
1 pt. red rhubarb cut in small pieces
1 c. sugar
juice and grated rind of ½ orange

Soak the gelatin in cold water. Cook the rhubarb with the sugar until the sauce is thick. Add the gelatin, and the juice and rind of the orange, beating the mixture well. When it is cold, place it between the layers of the cake and heap whipped cream on top.

Peanut Butter Crumb Cake

November 1934

A delicious cake which frosts itself. Suitable for lunch boxes or as a warm supper or coffee cake.

2 c. brown sugar
2½ c. sifted flour
½ tsp. salt
6 tbsp. butter
½ c. peanut butter
1 c. buttermilk
2 eggs, beaten
1 tsp. baking soda
1 tsp. vanilla

Mix together brown sugar, flour, and salt. Cut in both creamery butter and peanut butter with a dough blender or sharp-tined fork until like cornmeal. Take out ⅔ c. of this crumb mixture. To the rest add buttermilk, eggs, baking soda dissolved in 1 tsp. water, and vanilla. Beat and pour in greased pan. Sprinkle with crumbs. Bake in a moderate oven (375°F) about 30 minutes. This makes a large sheet cake or two round cakes.

Upside Down Strawberry Crumb Cake

June 1936

½ c. butter or part other fat
1 c. sugar
3 eggs, beaten
2 c. dry sifted breadcrumbs
½ c. flour
1 tsp. baking powder
⅛ tsp. salt
1 c. milk
½ tsp. almond extract

For Mold:
3 tbsp. melted butter
¾ c. brown sugar
fresh strawberries

Cream fat and sugar together thoroughly. Add eggs, then crumbs and dry ingredients alternately with milk and extract. Prepare mold or baking pan with melted butter, then sprinkle with sugar and whole or sliced strawberries to cover thickly. Pour on batter and bake in a moderate oven (350°F) for 40 minutes. When done, let stand a few minutes, unmold and cool. Serve with unsweetened whipped cream.

—*Mrs. G.A.C., Louisiana*

❧ Upside-Down Cake ❧

September 1938

When Kentucky farm women crave something different in the dessert line but do not have time to fix something fancy, they try upside-down cakes. They are easy to make and require but little time for preparation.

Even after the main part of your meal is cooking it is not too late to start an upside-down cake, stir it up, put it in the oven and let it bake while the rest of the meal is being eaten. And you may use your fruit "leftovers" to a good advantage.

The following recipe is one that has been successfully tried by women of rural Kentucky with different toppings.

Cake:

1½ c. flour

1 c. sugar

2 tsp. baking powder

½ tsp. salt

2 eggs broken into a cup which is then filled with rich milk or cream

1 tsp. vanilla

Sift dry ingredients together, add liquids and beat hard for five minutes. Set aside.

Pineapple Topping:
1 small can pineapple, crushed or sliced, ¾ c. juice reserved
4 tbsp. butter
¾ c. brown sugar

Place pineapple juice, brown sugar, and butter in a skillet. Bring to a boil and boil for 2 minutes. Place pineapple in the juice and cover with the batter, spreading it so it covers all the fruit. Bake in a moderately hot oven (375°F) for 30 minutes. Let stand until partly cool, turn upside down on cake plate or platter to serve. Accompany with unsweetened whipped cream.

It is essential to beat the batter until it is smooth and fluffy for a light cake of fine texture. In blending the brown sugar, butter, and fruit juice, do not boil the syrup until it becomes thick and candy-like. Let it boil only long enough to blend together well.

If you like a richer cake sprinkle a few nut meats in the syrup.

Orange Topping:
juice of one large orange
¾ c. brown sugar
4 tbsp. butter
2 oranges sliced in rings

Put juice, sugar, and butter in skillet. Bring to a boil. Slice the oranges in fairly thin rings and boil for 2 minutes. Arrange slices, overlapping if necessary, pour on batter. Bake in a moderate oven 35 to 40 minutes.

Spice Cake with Prune Topping

In the above cake recipe, omit vanilla and add ½ tsp. each allspice, cinnamon, and ground cloves, sifting them with the dry ingredients. For the topping use:

4 tbsp. butter
¾ c. brown sugar
¾ c. prune juice
2 c. cooked and pitted prunes, unsweetened

Boil sugar, juice, and butter for 2 minutes in a skillet. Place in prunes which have been well drained, with the uncut, skin side down. Pour in the batter and bake 30 minutes in a moderate oven.

"Mother, you're the bestes' cook in the whole world!"

What gives a mother greater pleasure than to make the kiddies happy with the goodies she prepares for them.

And how simple it is with a Monarch Range in your kitchen!

A Monarch oven is ready for any kind of baking in remarkably quick time—and with such little fuel.

A hot oven — a slow oven — a range that gives any service the occasion demands, and continues to do so for years to come.

To insure such service, the Monarch is built of unbreakable malleable iron, so it can be riveted—the only way to avoid air-leaks that cause fuel waste and cooking failures.

Investigate Now

There's no economy in using the old range even though it can be made to do for another year or so. Mail the coupon for information that will give you new ideas of what range service and economy should be.

Sour Milk Gingerbread

September 1934

2¾ c. flour
½ c. sugar
1½ tsp. baking powder
1 tsp. baking soda
½ tsp. salt
1 tsp. ground ginger
½ tsp. ground cloves
½ tsp. cinnamon
1 egg
1 c. buttermilk
1 c. molasses
¼ c. fat

Sift dry ingredients. Beat egg thoroughly, add buttermilk, molasses, and melted fat. Combine liquid and dry ingredients thoroughly. Pour into well-greased shallow pan. Bake 60 minutes at 325°F.

—*University of Minnesota*

Apple Gingerbread

May 1931

Pare, core, and slice several apples. Put in the bottom of a square or oblong pan and sprinkle with sugar. A very little water may be added. Put in moderate oven (350°F) to start cooking. When apples are partially cooked (15 to 20 minutes), pour over them a gingerbread batter (see preceding recipes), bake, and serve warm, with or without cream.

Blackberry-Gingerbread Cake

May 1931

Surprise your family with a berry upside-down cake, easy when one has canned blackberries in the cellar. Other berries or pitted cherries may be used.

2 c. flour
½ c. sugar
1 tsp. ginger
1 tsp. cinnamon
½ tsp. allspice
¼ tsp. salt
½ tsp. baking soda
1½ tsp. baking powder
1 egg
¾ c. molasses
¼ c. melted fat (shortening)
¾ c. hot water

Put all dry ingredients in a sifter. Put egg, molasses, shortening, and hot water in a bowl, sift in dry ingredients. Beat until well blended.

For the topping:
4 tbsp. butter
¾ c. berry juice
¾ c. brown sugar
2 c. berries, drained

In a skillet, bring butter, juice, and sugar to a boil and boil 2 minutes. Add berries, pour in batter carefully to cover all fruit. Bake in a moderate oven (350°F) for 35 minutes. Let stand in pan 15 minutes before turning out.

Hot Water Ginger Bread with Golden Cream

September 1928

2½ c. flour, measured after sifting
1 tsp. baking soda
1½ tsp. powdered ginger
½ tsp. salt
1 c. molasses
½ c. boiling water
4 tbsp. melted fat

Sift together the flour, baking soda, ginger, and salt. Combine the molasses, hot water, and fat, and stir into the dry ingredients. Beat vigorously. Pour into a shallow, greased pan, and bake in a moderate oven (350°F) for 25 to 30 minutes. Serve hot with:

Golden Cream:
1 egg yolk
1 c. whipped cream
½ c. confectioner's sugar

Beat the yolk, add the sugar, and fold into it the whipped cream. Flavor if desired (with 1 tsp. extract). Serve on the hot ginger bread.

❧ *Old, But Very Good* ❧

October 1928

Dear Editor: I am enclosing a recipe, which while an old one, is nevertheless, a very good one and a never-fail. People seem especially fond of this cake. A generous slice of it, with a cup of good coffee and a sandwich, makes a most excellent repast.

Spice Cake

1 c. butter
2 c. sugar (cream with butter)
3 eggs (break one at a time in batter and beat)
4 c. flour
2 tsp. baking powder (heaping)
vanilla
1 or 2 c. raisins
1 tsp. cloves (ground)
1 tsp. cinnamon
1 tsp. nutmeg
1 c. sweet milk

Beat well and bake in large dripping pan. (editor's note: Or, beat well and bake in an oiled cast iron skillet in a moderate oven (350°F).) Ice with the following:

Icing:
1 c. sugar and enough water—about ¼ c.—to melt, boiled together until the mixture threads. Cool a little and pour over stiffly beaten white of 1 egg, beating hard all the time.

—*Mrs. E.M.M., Oklahoma*

Fruit Roll

February 1933

1 pt. canned peaches mixed with:
½ tsp. ground cinnamon
½ c. brown sugar
1 tsp. lemon juice

Rich biscuit dough:
Mix and sift 2 c. flour, 3 tsp. baking powder, and 1 tsp. salt; quickly work in 4 tbsp. fat with a fork or dough blender. Add ⅔ c. milk all at once and stir lightly to make a soft dough. Turn out onto a slightly floured board, knead lightly for a few seconds.

Roll to ½ inch thickness, spread with seasoned peaches. Roll as for jelly roll. Bake in hot oven (425°F). Cut into individual servings. Serve with whipped cream.

—*A.B.M., Indiana*

Raspberry Roll

April 1926

Biscuit dough:
2 c. flour
3 tsp. baking powder
½ tsp. salt
2 tbsp. sugar
5 tbsp. fat
¾ to 1 c. milk

Sift dry ingredients and rub in fat. Add one-half cup of milk and stir lightly with knife until soft dough is formed. Remove to floured board, scrape together the remaining flour in the bowl and add enough milk to make a soft dough.

Filling:
1 pt. berries
1 c. sugar
1 tbsp. butter
1 c. hot water

Roll biscuit dough one-half inch thick; place berries in center and draw up ends like a dumpling or sprinkle with berries and roll like a jelly roll. Place in well-greased pan and sprinkle with 1 c. sugar. Dot with butter and pour one cup of boiling water over pudding. Cover closely and bake for about ½ an hour in moderate oven (350°F). Baste occasionally with the sugar and water, which will form a sauce to serve with the pudding.

Berry Roll

August 1929

Mix biscuit dough (see Raspberry Roll, above), roll thin, spread with blackberries. Sprinkle with sugar and butter and roll like a jelly roll. Put in pan, sprinkle top with sugar and bits of butter, and add water enough to make plenty of juice. Bake in moderate oven (400°F) until well done.

Apple Roly-Poly

February 1925

2 c. bread flour
5 tsp. baking powder
½ tsp. salt
2 tbsp. each butter and lard
⅔ to ¾ c. milk, depending on stiffening qualities of flour

Mix and sift dry ingredients, work in the fat and add milk to make dough to be handled as soft as possible. Turn on a floured board and pat into an oblong 1 inch thick. Brush with soft butter, sprinkle with 1 tbsp. sugar mixed with ½ tsp. cinnamon. Over this, sprinkle 3 or 4 sour apples which have been pared, cored, and chopped.

Roll like a jelly roll and cut into 8 slices. Place cut side up in a buttered acid-proof baking dish 2 inches deep, leaving a little space between them. Make the following brown sugar sauce and pour half of it over the dumplings. Bake 40 minutes at 350°F. Serve with other half of the sauce. Dried apples, soaked and chopped, may be used.

Brown Sugar Sauce:
¾ c. white sugar
½ c. light brown or maple sugar
1½ tbsp. flour
1½ c. boiling water
1½ tbsp. butter
¾ lemon, grated rind and juice

Mix and boil 6 minutes.

❧ *Complaint* ❧

November 1936

When Mother used to make a cake,
She'd pour the batter in a pan,
Then give the mixing crock to me
To "scrape"—and, Boy! O Man!

Now Mother has a rubber thing
She says works—to a "T"—
And uses it to scrape the crock
So clean there's nothing left for me!

—J. Earle Wycoff

Cupcakes

Buttermilk Cupcakes

October 1914

½ c. sugar, ½ c. butter, 1 egg beaten light, 1 c. buttermilk. Beat the first 3 ingredients together and in the buttermilk dissolve 1 tsp. baking soda, a little salt, ground cloves, allspice, and cinnamon to taste. Pour the buttermilk into the sugar and butter and add 1 c. molasses and 2 c. sifted flour. Bake in a moderate oven (350°F) in cupcake cups and frost with chocolate (try Easy Fudge Icing, page 104).

Plantation Cupcakes

April 1930

½ c. shortening
¼ c. brown sugar
2 eggs
½ c. molasses
1¾ c. sifted flour
¼ tsp. baking soda
1 tsp. baking powder
1 tsp. cinnamon
¼ tsp. mace
½ tsp. salt
½ c. milk

Cream the shortening and sugar together, and gradually work in the eggs, one at a time, until the mass is fluffy. Add the molasses. Mix and sift the dry ingredients, and add, alternately with the milk, until they are all blended. Bake in muffin pans (or paper cupcake cups) at about 350°F for 20 minutes.

Lemon
Sponge Cups

May 1938

2 tbsp. butter
1 c. sugar
¼ c. flour
pinch salt
grated rind of 1 lemon
⅓ c. lemon juice
3 eggs, separated
1½ c. milk

Cream butter, add sugar, flour, salt, and lemon rind and juice. Stir in egg yolks beaten with milk. Fold in stiffly beaten whites and pour in custard cups. Set cups in a pan of hot water. Bake 45 minutes at 350°F. When done, each cake will contain custard on the bottom.

Icings and Frostings

Chocolate Glaze

Semisweet chocolate
Butter

Melt chocolate with butter over simmering water, using 1 tbsp. butter for each ounce of chocolate. Allow to cool slightly before use.

Coffee Butter Icing

February 1936

⅓ c. butter
2 c. powdered sugar
1 or 2 tbsp. strong coffee
few drops vanilla

Soften butter by creaming and add sugar gradually. Add enough coffee to spread and then flavoring.

Comfort Icing

July 1933

2½ c. white sugar
½ to ¾ c. white corn syrup (use the smaller amount on a damp day)
½ c. water
2 egg whites

Boil sugar, syrup, and water together about 1 minute, then add 4 tbsp. of this syrup to the stiffly beaten egg whites, beating constantly. Cook remainder of syrup to firm ball stage (editor's note: 242°F registered on a candy thermometer) then add to egg white mixture and beat until it loses its shine and holds its shape (it need not be beaten constantly, just often enough to prevent a crust from forming over the top). The icing may be used immediately or stored in a covered jar. It keeps 4 to 6 weeks in a cool place. When putting the stored icing on a cake, add a few drops of hot water so that the icing will be just thin enough to spread. It sets quickly and does not become dry and crumbly.

100

Boiled Icing I

May 1927

2 c. granulated sugar
⅓ c. water and ¼ tsp. cream of tartar

Boil until it spins a thread when droped from the tip of a spoon.

Pour very slowly over beaten whites of 2 eggs.

Spread over the filling and ice sides of cakes.

Boiled Icing II

December 1925

1¾ c. sugar
¾ c. boiling water
3 egg whites
1 tsp. any desired extract
1 level tsp. baking powder

Reserve 1½ tbsp. sugar. Dissolve remaining sugar in boiling water—if cover is placed over saucepan for a few minutes it will prevent sugar from adhering to the sides of pan. Let this boil very rapidly. When heavy drops fall from a spoon when spoon is held high above saucepan, then it is time to beat egg whites—a tiny pinch of salt may be added to whites before beginning to beat. Wait until syrup begins to thicken before beating egg whites because if beaten egg whites stand, they will liquefy.

When eggs are well beaten, add the reserved sugar and beat well into egg whites until stiff but not dry.

Test boiling syrup again. If it silks to a long thread which flies out, it is ready to be poured very slowly over beaten egg whites mixed with extract—beating vigorously. After beating about 5 minutes, add baking powder. Continue beating until it is cool and you have a smooth, creamy filling which should stand up well.

Boiled Icing III

June 1928

1 c. white sugar
½ c. brown sugar
½ c. ground nut meats
½ c. thick cream
lump of butter the size of a walnut

Boil all together until it threads when droped from the tip of a spoon. Set in a pan of cold water until it begins to set, then beat until the right consistency to spread on the cake.

Boiled Marshmallow Icing

February 1939

2½ c. granulated sugar
½ c. light corn syrup
¼ tsp. salt
½ c. water
2 egg whites
1 tsp. vanilla
8 marshmallows, cut in quarters

Cook sugar, corn syrup, salt, and water together in a saucepan to the firm ball stage (editor's note: 250°F registered on a candy thermometer). Pour the hot syrup slowly into the well-beaten egg whites, beating constantly. Add vanilla extract and continue beating until the frosting will hold its shape when tossed over the back of a spoon. Add marshmallows.

Seven-Minute Icing

February 1939

1 c. sugar
1 egg white
¼ c. water
1 tbsp. syrup or honey
few grains salt
½ tsp. vanilla

Put all ingredients except vanilla in the top of a double boiler. Cook over boiling water 7 to 10 minutes, beating all the while with a rotary beater. When ready to remove from the stove, the icing will be thick and almost ready to spread. Add vanilla, beat until cool and ready to spread. Double the recipe for all but a small cake.

Caramel Nut Icing

February 1936

2 c. sugar
1 c. thin sweet or sour cream
3 tbsp. caramel syrup★
1 tbsp. butter
1 tsp. grated orange rind
nut meats

Boil sugar, cream, and syrup until the mixture forms a soft ball in cold water (candy thermometer reading of 234–240). Remove from fire, let cool, add butter and grated orange rind, and beat until thick and creamy. Spread on cake. Decorate top with whole nut meats.

★Caramel syrup. Make a syrup by melting 2 c. white sugar in a smooth, heavy skillet until golden brown. Avoid overheating or the syrup will have a burned taste. Add 1 c. hot water, stir until caramel is dissolved, and boil until a heavy syrup. Cool, store in a jar until needed.

Icing for Petit Fours

April 1931

¼ c. butter
4 c. confectioner's sugar
1 egg yolk
½ c. whipped cream
½ tsp. vanilla

Cream butter until light and very fluffy. Add some of the sugar, gradually creaming it in. Add well-beaten egg yolk and more sugar, then the whipped cream and gradually the rest of the sugar and vanilla. Divide the icing into 4 parts and color each differently.

Easy Fudge Icing

February 1936

2 tbsp. softened butter
1 whole egg or 2 yolks
few grains of salt
1 square melted unsweetened chocolate
½ tsp. vanilla
2 c. powdered sugar
cream as necessary

Put first 4 ingredients in bowl and beat with rotary beater until creamy. Add vanilla and powdered sugar and enough cream to spread easily. Put on with even strokes, leaving a slightly ridged appearance.

Allegretti Icing

January 1914

Boil 1 c. sugar and ½ c. water until it will form a soft ball when dropped in cold water (editor's note: 234°F to 240°F registered on a candy thermometer). Pour this very gradually on the stiffly beaten white of an egg. Beat until it is the right consistency to spread on the cake, let this icing harden on the cake, then melt 2 squares sweetened chocolate and spread over the white icing. The chocolate prevents the white icing from becoming too hard and cracking when the cake is cut, and also adds delicacy to the cake.

Orange Icing
January 1914

Beat the white of 1 egg until very stiff, add the juice and pulp of 1 orange and mix with enough confectioner's sugar to make it the right consistency for spreading. Cover the top and sides of the cake with the icing.

Chocolate Butter Frosting
July 1933

4 tbsp. butter
2 c. sifted confectioner's sugar
½ tsp. vanilla
1½ squares unsweetened chocolate, melted
4 tsp. milk

Cream butter, add 1 c. sugar and cream together thoroughly. Add vanilla and chocolate. Add remaining sugar gradually, beating well after each addition. Thin with milk until of the right consistency to spread. Makes enough frosting to cover top of 8x8-inch cake, or tops of two 9-inch layers.

Cherry Frosting
February 1936

1 c. sugar
½ c. water
⅛ tsp. cream of tartar
1 egg white, beaten
few drops almond flavoring
⅓ c. drained chopped cherries (preserved or maraschino)

Put sugar, water, and cream of tartar in a saucepan to cook, stirring until dissolved. Then cook without stirring until the syrup spins a good thread (editor's note: 240°F registered on a candy thermometer). Pour over egg white slowly, beating meanwhile. Add flavoring and cherries which must be well drained of extra juice or the frosting will be too soft. Continue to beat until thick and ready to spread.

—*A.A.F., Wisconsin*

Luscious Lemon Frosting
May 1938

1 tbsp. grated orange rind
3 tbsp. butter
3 c. sifted confectioner's sugar
2 tbsp. lemon juice
1 tbsp. water
dash of salt

Add orange rind to butter; cream well. Add part of sugar gradually, stirring after each addition. Combine lemon juice and water; add to creamed mixture, alternating with remaining sugar, until of right consistency to spread. Beat after each addition until smooth. Add salt. Makes enough frosting to cover tops and sides of two 8-inch layers (generously) or top and sides of 8x8x2-inch cake (generously) or about 3 dozen cupcakes.

Pies, Tarts, and Other Pastries

❧ Perfections in Pie Making ❧
On the Farm This Dessert Should Shine in All Its Glory

By Annette Chase Dimock, April 1923

Anyone who has ever lived on a farm can see why farming and pies make a natural combination. A man doing heavy muscular work wants a palatable, sizable dessert that will give the feeling of satisfaction that mere bulk does and that will "stay by." On the other hand, people who use the brain more and muscles less find pie a dietetic sin.

Pastry is made of flour, fat, salt and just enough water to hold these together as they are rolled out.

None of the ingredients of pastry are unwholesome in themselves but the mixture of fat plus starch may prevent starch digestion beginning in the mouth as it should, so digestion is retarded, especially if the pie is not masticated thoroughly.

Either pastry or bread flour may be used for pie crust. Some pie-makers think that pastry flour is easier to use and more economical. A good substitute for pastry flour is made by using 2 level tbsp. corn-starch to each c. of bread flour. If bread flour alone is used, to avoid a tough crust, never use less than 1⅛ c. fat to 4 c. flour.

The fat used may be lard, any of the various "hardened vegetable fats" or "compounds," drippings, chicken fat, tried-out suet, vegetable oil (corn, cottonseed, peanut), butter. A good crust may be made with cream if the cook is expert. A mixture of fats may be used. Butter alone may be too expensive to have many advocates. The sweetness of flavor of whatever fat is used is the important thing. If butter is used, allowance must be made for the water and other substances which it contains. If oils alone are used, never allow more than 4 tbsp. to 1 c. flour.

The Size of the Pie Tins

If a pie plate is only 7 or 8 inches in diameter, 1 c. flour will be sufficient for 2 crusts.

If the pie plate is 9 inches in diameter, use 1½ c. flour.

If the plate is over 9 inches, use 1⅔ c. flour

A 1-crust pie requires little more than half the amount for 2 crusts.

3. 6. 4. 5. 2.

Pie Crusts

Plain Pastry— 2 Crusts
1934

½ tsp. salt
1½ c. sifted flour
½ c. lard
3 or 4 tbsp. ice cold water

Add salt to flour and cut in shortening with a dough blender, sharp-tined fork, or finger tips, until pieces are size of small peas. Add a little water at a time, mixing with a fork lightly until it can be shaped into a ball. Divide dough and roll out 1 crust at a time. Avoid overhandling the dough either in mixing it or in rolling out the crust. Work quickly, especially in warm weather so that fat doesn't melt. To bake single crusts, lay in pie tin quite loosely and prick well over bottom or fit over the bottom of an inverted tin. Bake in a hot oven (450°F).

Tough crust may be due to too much water and too little fat, overhandling, or too slow an oven. Soggy undercrust may be due to not having the oven hot enough to bake the under crust before the filling soaks in, or to having the crust so rich or rolled so thin that the filling breaks through.

Hot Water Pastry— 2 Crusts
1934

½ to ⅔ c. lard
¼ c. boiling water
1½ c. flour
½ tsp. salt
½ tsp. baking powder

Warm a bowl, put in shortening, add boiling water and beat until creamy. Sift in dry ingredients; mix well. Chill, then roll out into 2 crusts. This makes a rather mealy, rich crust but not flaky in texture. The inexperienced cook will find it easy to make. The dough must be chilled before it can be rolled; hence it is not practical in hot weather without good refrigeration.

Pie with 1 Crust

April 1923

This is unbaked, before filling and is suitable for custard, pumpkin, squash, and sour cream pies.

Select a deep dish pie plate. Some good cooks use a sheet iron frying pan for such pies. Take a little more than half the crust required for Plain Pastry—2-Crusts (page 110). Roll it into a round sheet that will come about ¾ inch beyond the edge of the plate. Place crust evenly on the plate, lifting it here and there to be sure that all air escapes. Air bubbles left under 1-crust pies expand in baking and force the filling out of the plate.

Fold the edge under to meet the plate and flute this double fold of pastry with the thumb and finger. Press each fluting down upon the edge of the plate.

For this kind of pie, many cooks like to use tried-out suet, wholly or in part, because it makes a firmer pastry which will best hold a given shape. (To make your own tried-out suet, cut suet into small piece and place in a moderately hot oven until fat is "tried out," or rendered. Strain before use.)

To Make Flaky Pastry

April 1923

Have all ingredients very cold. Pat and roll the pastry in rectangular shape. Spread with ½ tbsp. fat. Fold to make 3 layers. Pat gently with rolling pin, then roll up like jelly roll. Butter is often used for this dressing-up process. To make it spread easily, wash it in cold water to remove all buttermilk and to make it waxy and pliable. Pat in a cloth to remove excess moisture before spreading. Pastry may be wrapped in wax paper (to keep from drying out) and kept in a cool place for several days.

Susanna's Everyday Pie Crust

April 1923

Sift and weigh 5 lbs. flour. Into this sift 5 level tsp. baking powder and 6 level tsp. salt. Then cut, chop, or work into the mixture with cold fingers, 2½ lbs. lard or other fat.

A little baking powder insures lightness and gives a mealy rather than a flaky quality which my family likes.

❦ When Thea Bakes ❦

By Eva K. Anglesburg, October 1935

When Thea bakes I swear she makes
White magic, for the pies and cakes
That she creates could never be
Achieved except by sorcery.
Some few ingredients she takes
And these she whisks and creams and flakes
Till my poor heart with envy aches

At her transcendent artistry;
When Thea bakes.

Far, far too freely one partakes
And soon without a qualm forsakes
Long cherished slimness willingly
For softly cushioned curves . . . Ah me,
That such an appetite awakes.
When Thea bakes.

Everyday Pies

Angel Pie

April 1939

Crust:
6 tbsp. butter
1 c. flour
3 tbsp. sugar

Filling:
¾ c. sugar
3 tbsp. cornstarch
1 c. hot water
1 lemon, juice and grated rind
3 egg whites
¼ tsp. salt
⅓ c. whipping cream
⅓ c. crushed peanut brittle

Blend together softened butter, flour, and sugar. Put into a pie pan and bake 15 minutes in a moderately hot oven (400°F). Cool. For the filling, combine sugar and cornstarch, add hot water and cook 10 minutes, stirring until thick. Add grated rind of lemon, cool slightly, add juice. Fold in whites beaten until stiff with salt. Pour in shell and let stand until firm. Spread top with whipped cream and sprinkle with crushed peanut brittle. (Or a color scheme may be carried out with the use of other crushed candy.)

Washington Pie
March 1913

Make the crusts by beating the yolks of 6 eggs very light, add 2 c. fine sugar and mix again, add 3 c. flour sifted with 2 tsp. cream of tartar, mix well and add the stiffly beaten egg whites of the 6 eggs, and 1 tsp. baking soda dissolved in 2 tbsp. sweet milk.

Bake in 3 pie pans at 400°F, then fill with the following custard: 2 c. thick milk, let it come to the boiling point, and add 2 well-beaten eggs, 1 c. sugar, and 1 c. flour. Stir until quite thick, flavor with vanilla. Cool.

Vinegar Pie
October 1913

1 c. sugar, ½ c. vinegar, 3 tbsp. flour, 1 tsp. cinnamon, 2 c. water. Boil until it thickens in a double boiler. Pour into baked crust and bake at 350°F. When nearly done, spread over the whites of 2 eggs, well beaten. This is enough for 1 pie.

Cottage Cheese Pie I
October 1933

⅔ c. milk
½ c. sugar (combined with the flour)
2 tbsp. flour
1 egg yolk, beaten
1 c. cottage cheese
2 tbsp. butter
1 lemon, juice and grated rind

Heat milk, add slowly to the sugar and flour which have been combined, then return to the top part of double boiler and cook mixture until thick, stirring it constantly. Add the yolk and cook the mixture until the egg thickens. Add cheese, butter, and lemon. Pour into well-baked crust. Cover with meringue (see page 123) and brown in slow oven (300°F).

Part of the filling from the cottage cheese pie can be saved out for small Judy for dessert. Or, if you dislike making pie crust, the filling may be put in a baking dish, topped with meringue, browned in the oven, and served. It really is tasty and a good way to give the family more milk products.

❧ From "Perfections in ❧ Pie Making—On the Farm This Dessert Should Shine in All Its Glory"

by Annette Chase Dimock, April 1923

To Prevent Juice from Running Out

1. Fit lower crust loosely on the plate.
2. Do not stretch upper crust over the filling—make sure it fits easily.
3. Before adjusting upper crust, moisten the edge of the lower crust preferably with milk or water.
4. Fold upper crust so that about ⅛ inch projects over lower crust. Carefully press together. Put the projecting "lap" over the edge of the lower crust inside the tin and press down. Then pinch in fancy rim with thumbs and fingers.
5. Beginners are safer if they cut the 2 crusts evenly, after pinching together and then binding edge of plate and pie with a strip of white cloth—cut 1 inch wide—wet with cold water, or with parchment pie tape.
6. Make a small funnel of brown paper and stick the small end (½ inch) in a small opening in the center of the upper crust. To Prevent Undercrusts from Soaking

1. Start the baking in a hot oven to cook the undercrust before it becomes moist, then reduce the heat.
2. Brush pastry with white of egg.
3. Dredge pastry with flour.
4. Before adding very moist filling like custard, bake the lower crust about 5 minutes or until it just begins to color.
5. Before filling, allow the shells to stand in the air for a few hours to dry.

Cottage Cheese Pie II

November 1931

Another pie due to its tartness and appetizing quality especially good for holiday time on the farm.

2 c. cottage cheese
1 tbsp. cornstarch
½ tsp. salt
½ c. butter
1 c. sugar
juice and grated rind of 1 lemon
3 eggs, separated

Put the cottage cheese through a sieve or mash finely. Add the cornstarch and salt, also the butter creamed with the sugar. Then the lemon juice and rind. Beat in the egg yolks one at a time and then fold in the beaten egg whites.

Pour into an unbaked pie shell. Bake in a hot oven (450°F) for 10 minutes, then reduce the temperature to 350°F and bake about 30 minutes, until the filling is set.

Honey Cheese Pie

1934

2 eggs, beaten
1 c. cottage cheese, sieved until fine
½ c. honey
juice and grated rind of ½ lemon
unbaked pastry to line an 8-inch pie tin
½ c. graham cracker crumbs
1 tbsp. butter
1 tbsp. sugar

Add eggs to cottage cheese, and then add honey and lemon juice and rind. Mix well and pour into pan lined with unbaked pastry. Sprinkle with topping of graham cracker crumbs mixed with butter and sugar. Bake in very moderate oven (325°F to 350°F) for 25 minutes.

Shoo-Fly "Cake"
February 1937

2 pastry-lined tins (Plain Pastry, for example, page 110)
2½ c. sifted flour
2 c. brown sugar
½ c. butter or part other fat
1 c. molasses
1 c. hot water
1 scant tsp. baking soda
sprinkle salt

Mix flour, 1 c. brown sugar, and butter to make crumbs. Mix molasses, hot water, baking soda, and other cup of brown sugar. Sprinkle a layer of crumbs in bottom of each pastry-lined tin, then pour in half of liquid. Add a few more crumbs, rest of liquid, then top with crumbs. Bake in moderate oven (350°F) until firm.

Butterscotch Pie I
1934

2 c. milk
6 tbsp. flour
1½ c. brown sugar
1/8 tsp. salt
2 egg yolks, beaten
3 tbsp. butter
1 tsp. vanilla
meringue (see page 123)

Scald milk; add flour, sugar, and salt, stirred to a smooth paste in a little cold milk. Cook 15 minutes in a double boiler. Add a little of the hot mixture to yolks, then return yolk mixture to mixture in the double boiler and cook 2 to 3 minutes. Add butter and flavoring. Pour into baked crust. Cover with meringue. Bake 20 minutes at 350°F.

Butterscotch Pie II

May 1931

1 c. brown sugar
2 tbsp. flour
2 eggs yolks, beaten
⅛ tsp. salt
1 tbsp. melted butter
1 tsp. vanilla
1 c. sour cream

Mix ingredients together and pour into an unbaked pie crust. Bake for 10 minutes in a hot oven (450°F). Reduce heat to 350°F and bake until an inserted knife comes out clean. When nearly done, top with a meringue made with:

2 beaten egg whites
4 tbsp. sugar

Return to the oven to brown.

Chess Pie

April 1931

8 egg yolks
3 c. white sugar
¼ c. cream
1 tsp. vanilla or lemon extract
rich pastry crust (such as Flaky Pastry, page 112) in muffin tins

Mix together in order given. Fill unbaked pie crusts. Bake in slow oven (300°F) for 20 minutes to ½ hour.

—*Mrs. D., Tennessee*

Buttermilk Pie

September 1934

2 tbsp. butter
2 tbsp. flour
2 egg yolks + 1 whole egg
1½ c. sugar
1 tbsp. lemon juice
2½ c. buttermilk
meringue (see page 123)

Cream the butter and flour together. Add the beaten yolks and egg. Add sugar, lemon juice, and buttermilk, stirring well. Pour into pie plates lined with **(unbaked)** rich pastry and bake at 450°F for 10 minutes before lowering to 350°F. Use 2 leftover egg whites for meringue.

—*Mrs. S. G. P., Wisconsin*

Chocolate Pie

1934

2 squares unsweetened chocolate, cut
1 pt. rich milk
3 tbsp. flour
¾ c. sugar
few grains salt
2 egg yolks, beaten
1 tsp. vanilla
baked pie shell
meringue (see page 123)

Scald chocolate and milk in double boiler; add flour, ½ c. of the sugar and salt well mixed. Cook 15 minutes until flour is well cooked. Add yolks beaten with the remaining ¼ c. of sugar. Stir quickly until thickened. Remove from fire, add vanilla, cool slightly, and pour into baked shell. Cover with meringue and bake 20 minutes. If pie is to be topped with whipped cream, decrease flour to 2 tbsp. and use 2 whole eggs.

Cream Pie

1934

2 c. rich milk
½ c. sugar
¼ c. cornstarch or ⅓ c. flour
¼ tsp. salt
2 egg yolks, beaten
1 tsp. vanilla
meringue (see page 123)

Scald 1¾ c. milk in top of double boiler. Mix remaining ¼ c. milk with sugar, cornstarch, and salt and add to milk. Cook 10 minutes, stirring constantly. Add egg yolks to mixture, stirring a little of the hot custard into eggs first. Cook 3 to 5 minutes; add vanilla and cool slightly. Pour in baked shell, cover with meringue and bake 20 minutes at 425°F.

Variations:

Banana Cream Pie: Slice bananas into baked shell, pour on custard and finish as directed.

Strawberry or Pineapple Cream Pie: Fresh sliced strawberries or canned pineapple may be used in place of bananas.

Cream Pies

❧ Pies for a Week ❧
If You Have a Large Family, This Will Help

By Ina B. Rowe

The housewife will save some valuable time if she will schedule her pies for a week in advance and do most of the work for them on one of her least busy mornings. The two-crust juicy pies which are to be used at once, mince pie which may be reheated, and pie shells to be filled when needed, all may be made and baked in one morning and whatever paste is left over will keep for several days if put in a cool place. One can make the paste for a dozen pies almost as quickly as for one, and the saving by preparing a quantity at a time is very appreciable.

Two quarts of flour will be ample for 12 8-inch, single-crust pies. On that basis the recipe is as follows:

2 level tbsp. salt
3½ c. shortening
2 qts. flour
cold water to make dough

Work the fat into the salt and flour lightly with the tips of the fingers. Too vigorous mixing toughens the crust and if the lard is too finely divided the crust will be less flaky. The amount of water cannot be definitely stated because different flours differ in hardness and very cold ingredients require more water than warm. Pour the water a little at a time into small wells made in the mixed flour and fat. Lift the dry ingredients through the water on the tips of the fingers, being careful not to knead the dough. When the dough is sufficiently moist it will clean the sides of the mixing bowl. Stop at this point and handle each pie from then on separately. Materials and utensils should at all times be kept as cold as possible.

A simple cream filling for the shells is made as follows:

¾ c. sugar
¼ c. flour
2 c. milk

| 3 egg yolks |
| 1 tbsp. butter |
| 1 tsp. vanilla |
| ¼ tsp. salt |

Mix the sugar and flour. Stir in the milk and cook until the mixture thickens and the starchy taste disappears. Remove from the fire and add the beaten egg yolks, butter, vanilla, and salt, stirring rapidly. This is merely a foundation cream filling which may be varied indefinitely.

<h3 style="text-align:center">Variations of cream filling:</h3>

Add 1 c. of shredded coconut.

Slice a banana in the bottom of the shell and stir over it the cream filling.

Spread a layer of sliced oranges in the shell and add one tbsp. orange juice and the grated rind of an orange to the filling. Pour the filling over the oranges.

Drain the juice completely from 1 c. of shredded pineapple. When making the filling use the juice thus drained off in place of an equal amount of milk for additional flavor. Stir in the drained pineapple and place in the shell.

Caramelize 4 tbsp. of granulated sugar and add to it 4 tbsp. of boiling water. When blended, add to the cream filling.

Substitute brown or maple sugar for the white.

Melt 2 squares of chocolate with ¼ c. of sugar and 2 tbsp. of water. When smooth, add to the cream filling.

When the fillings are in the shells, cover with meringue and bake in a medium oven (350°F) until nicely browned.

<h3 style="text-align:center">Meringue</h3>

| 2 egg whites |
| 2 tbsp. sugar |
| ¼ tsp. vanilla |

Beat the whites until stiff but not dry. Add sugar and beat until smooth and glossy. Add vanilla, spread on top of pie and bake.

Delicious Cream Pie

June 1934

½ c. granulated sugar
2 level tbsp. flour
⅛ tsp. salt
1 pint cream
1 tsp. vanilla
2 egg whites beaten stiff
unbaked pie shell

Mix dry ingredients and gradually stir cream into it. Add vanilla and last the whites of eggs. Mix thoroughly. Pour into unbaked pie shell and bake in a moderate oven until well set. Be sure not to let boil. These are delicious when cooled.

—Mrs. R.D., Indiana

The Farmer's Wife food editor's note: A chilled crust and warm filling help keep the crust crisp. This pie has a perfect texture and flavor when properly baked.

Cocoanut Cream Pie

October 1931

unbaked pie pastry (such as for Flaky Pastry, page 112)
2 c. milk or cocoanut milk
2 eggs, separated
¼ tsp. salt
3 tbsp. sugar
1 c. grated unsweetened cocoanut

Line a pie tin with uncooked pie pastry, add filling mixture made with milk, egg yolks, salt, sugar, and cocoanut as in regular custards. Bake at 450°F for 10 minutes then reduce heat to moderate (350°F) and continue cooking for 30 minutes. Make meringue with left-over egg whites (see page 123). Spread on top of pie, bake until golden brown.

—Mrs. Nora Townner

Plum Cream Pie

July 1929

Line deep tins with good flaky crust dough and fill them with very ripe, peeled, seeded plums. Add a slight dusting of flour, a cup or so of sugar—according to the type of plum—a sprinkle of cinnamon and little, if any, water; bake in a moderate oven (350°F) until fruit is tender. Remove and cool and pile thick with sweetened whipped cream that is mixed with chipped marshmallows. This may be made of canned plums as well.

Apple Cream Pie

October 1929

For crust:
Take 1 c. of flour, 1 egg, 1½ tsp. baking powder, ¼ tsp. salt, 2 tbsp. sugar, and enough sweet cream to make a soft dough. Roll out a little thicker than other pie crust.

Filling:
Fill crust ⅔ full with diced cooking apples. Add following mixture: 1 c. sour cream, 1 egg, 1 tbsp. flour, 1 c. sugar. Dust with cinnamon and bake in moderate oven (375°F). Peaches or cherries may be used in place of apples.

—*Mrs. E.P.R., Nebraska*

Cherry Cream Pie

June 1910

Line a plate with nice pastry, add 2 c. stoned cherries, 1 c. sugar, and bake at 400°F until nearly done, then pour over it 1 egg beaten light and mixed with ½ c. rich sweet cream, return to oven at 375°F and finish baking, until the custard is set.

Fruit Pies

Fresh Fruit Pie
1934

¼ to ⅓ c. flour
1 to 1½ c. sugar
¼ tsp. salt
1 qt. fruit (washed and prepared)
2 tbsp. butter

Thoroughly mix flour, sugar, and salt. (Use smaller amounts of sugar and flour with sweet fruits.) Mix this with fruit and turn into pie tin lined with unbaked pastry. Dot with butter. Put ½-inch strips of pastry, lattice fashion, over the top. Bake 15 minutes in a hot oven (450°F) and then in a moderate oven (350°F) for remainder of baking.

Fruits such as blueberries, gooseberries, peaches, rhubarb, and cherries may be used. Two good combinations: Equal parts currants and huckleberries; or 5 sliced tart apples with a few huckleberries tossed in.

French Apple Pie
August 1931

18 graham crackers
¼ c. sugar
½ c. soft (not melted) butter
2 c. apple sauce

Roll crackers fine. Mix to a moist paste with sugar and butter. (Add no liquid.) Pat the mixture in a pie tin, pressing down firmly on bottom and on sides as if using pastry dough. Add the filling of 2 c. apple sauce, sweetened with sugar and seasoned with cinnamon. Sprinkle cracker crumbs on top. Dot with butter. Pour on hot milk until you can see it rising around the sides. Bake 1¼ hours in moderate (350°F) oven.

Favorite Pie

October 1913

Peel 6 common-sized tart apples and stew; while hot, stir in 1 tbsp. butter. Beat yolks of 3 eggs and 1 c. sugar together. Add 1 c. sweet cream, 2 tbsp. cornstarch, and the apples, smashed. Add juice of 1 lemon or lemon extract to taste. Bake in a good pie crust (unbaked) in a moderate oven (375°F) until nearly done and spread over the top the egg whites well beaten and sweetened. Return to oven to brown. This is for 2 large pies.

Cherry Pie

June 1910

Cook 2 c. stoned cherries with 1 c. sugar and ½ c. water until a rich preserve. Line a plate with a rich unbaked pastry, fill with cherries, bake (400°F) until the crust is done, and serve with whipped cream piled on top.

Champion Cherry Pie

March 1936

2½ c. drained sour cherries
1 c. sugar
⅛ tsp. salt
2½ tbsp. quick-cooking tapioca
1/3 c. cherry juice
1 tsp. butter

Drain cherries. Mix sugar, salt, tapioca, and juice only; let stand while mixing pastry for 2-crust pie (such as Plain Pastry, page 110). Line a tin with lower crust. Add drained cherries to juice mixture and pour in crust. Dot with butter. Cut top crust to allow for escape of steam. Put on top crust and bake at 450°F for 10 minutes, then 350°F for 25 minutes. Cool before serving.

—*Inez Todnem, Marshall, Minnesota*

Cheers for Cherry Pies

May 1938

One cheer goes for the good-looking cooks themselves—eight of them from eight different states—who entered this national cherry pie baking contest held recently in Chicago.

A second cheer goes for the delectable pies which these girls baked from cherries grown and canned in their states. Flaky brown crusts bursting with cherry-red fruit and oozing a bit of crimson juice! That tart-sweet flavor of cherries enhanced with a bit of butter and a meltingly-rich pastry!

A third cheer goes to the country kitchen cooks among them, for six of eight got their start in pie baking in a kitchen whose windows framed a view of the red barn and silo or perhaps a wheat field or cherry orchard.

Here are recipes for . . . three different fillings, each distinctive in its own way. You will notice that all of the recipes call for unsweetened canned red cherries, drained. Drain first, then measure cherries and juice as directed.

Indiana Cherry Pie

3 tbsp. cornstarch (5 tbsp. if pie will be served warm)
½ c. juice
1 c. sugar
1 tbsp. butter
few grains salt
3 c. unsweetened red canned cherries, drained

Mix cornstarch and juice in top of double boiler. Cook until thick, stirring constantly. Add sugar and cook 5 minutes longer. Remove from fire, add butter and salt, then cherries, stirring carefully. Let stand while the crust is mixed and rolled (such as Plain Pastry—2-Crusts, page 110), pour into pastry-lined tin. Cover with top crust, and cut to allow for escape of steam. Seal edges, bake 15 minutes in a hot oven (425°F) and 30 minutes in a moderate oven (350°F).

—*Mary Wien, Indiana*

Ohio Cherry Pie

3 c. drained, unsweetened canned cherries

1 c. sugar

sprinkle salt

2 tbsp. flour

¼ c. juice

Line plate with pastry (such as Plain Pastry—2-Crusts, page 110). Sprinkle bottom crust with a little flour. Spread half of cherries in, then sprinkle over them half of the sugar, salt, and flour mixed well together. Cover with remaining cherries and juice, and rest of sugar mixture on top. Put on upper crust. Brush top with milk, then sprinkle lightly with sugar. Bake at 425°F for 10 minutes, then reduce heat to 350°F and bake 30 to 40 minutes longer, till crust is nicely golden and filling is set.

—*Eleanor Enos, Ohio*

Michigan Cherry Pie

3 c. cherries, canned without sugar, drained

1 c. juice

1¼ c. sugar

3½ tbsp. cornstarch

2 tbsp. butter

½ tsp. almond extract

Mix cherries, cherry juice, and sugar. Allow to stand 5 minutes while crust is being made (such as Plain Pastry—2-Crusts, page 110). Drain juice from cherries. Mix cornstarch with a little of the juice until smooth. Bring remaining juice to a boil; stir in cornstarch mixture. Boil, stirring constantly, for 1 minute. Remove, add butter. Let cool until crust is rolled out. Add cherries and almond extract to thickened juice; pour into pastry shell. Adjust top crust; press down edge with tines of a fork. Cut off excess pastry. Bake in a hot oven (425°F) until crust is golden brown, about 45 minutes.

—*Annabelle Jones, Michigan*

Variation:

To any of the cherry pie recipes above, substitute 1 c. blueberries or raspberries for 1 c. cherries.

Can You make a *Cherry Pie* as "PERFECT" as this One?

In a recent test it was found that only 4 out of 149 Women could make a really perfect cherry pie

BETTY CROCKER
has originated literally hundreds of recipes.

THAT'S WHY BETTY CROCKER GIVES YOU HER RECIPE IN THE SACKS OF THIS FLOUR!

(ABOVE) Actual color photograph of Betty Crocker's "PERFECT" Cherry Pie. Cherries oozing out. Makes your mouth water merely to look at it!

"CAN she bake a Cherry Pie, Billy Boy, Billy Boy?" So run the words of the old song.

We asked 149 women to bake cherry pies for us. We wanted to know whether the average woman who bakes at home could bake a really perfect cherry pie ... when she used her own recipe and *"any flour she happened to have"* (exclusive of Gold Medal). Then we had these pies judged by domestic science experts.

Only 4 of the 149 were perfect! Most had minor flaws such as crusts which weren't flaky enough ... and many were soggy and of poor shape. Only four were as perfect as the Betty Crocker pie shown here.

That's why we include Betty Crocker's Cherry Pie recipe in the sacks of Gold Medal Flour this month.

In a recent survey of nation-wide scope the majority of home economists replying stated that flour is the most important single factor in baking success *(apart of course from the recipe itself)* ...

That is why we believe you are foolish to risk the use of a cheap, untested flour in your baking.

For such a flour is liable to act wrong just when you least want it to ... with disastrous results to whatever you may be making at the time! Gold

Medal Flour, on the other hand, cannot go wrong because it is milled by millers with the largest aggregate experience in the business—*then tested out by Betty Crocker and her staff of experts to give perfect baking results!*

Use GOLD MEDAL *"Kitchen-tested"* Flour always. It is one of the best possible forms of insurance against costly baking "mistakes."

Get a sack of Gold Medal *"Kitchen-tested"* Flour today!

Why More Women Use Gold Medal than Any Other Brand of Flour!

EACH SACK of Gold Medal Flour is the result of 150 separate steps from the wheat to the finished product.

The wheat is first selected from the finest wheat counties in America. Then the grain is carefully milled in a total of 115 different operations. Different "streams" of flour are

blended so assure perfect results. Then the flour is "laboratory" tested and tested in Betty Crocker's kitchens for making cakes, pies, bread, etc.

This explains—we believe—why more women use Gold Medal Flour than any other. It has been used by generations of homemakers.

IN THE SACKS! Every month the sacks of Gold Medal *"Kitchen-tested"* Flour contain a different twine folder .... This month's folder shown above. Contains variety of recipes. Forthcoming folders include recipes for: Chocolate Cream Cake, Molasses Crinkles, Sunshine Cake, etc. Also Silverware coupon and Baking Hints.

$10 WILL BE PAID for each of these recipes using Gold Medal Flour sent us before Aug. 1st, which Betty Crocker considers now interesting, unusual and practical. Send us your recipe *(no prizes returned).* Address BETTY CROCKER, Dept. 169, Minneapolis, Minnesota.

Makes fine-textured bread!

IMPROVE QUALITY OF ANY BREAD OR ROLLS YOU BAKE

Breads should rise sufficiently, have a fine texture, a golden-brown tender crust and a clear white crumb quality and nutty flavor. ... Gold Medal gives you bread of this quality. *It is tested in making bread daily!*

Gold Medal "*Kitchen-Tested*" Flour

Copyright 1938, General Mills, Inc.

"Kitchen-tested" is a reg. Trade mark of General Mills, Inc.

Lattice-Top Strawberry- Cherry Pie

June 1936

1 c. fresh strawberries, sliced
1½ c. sour red cherries, drained and ¼ c. of juice reserved
2½ tbsp. fine tapioca
1 c. sugar
dash of salt
1 tsp. butter

Combine reserved cherry juice, tapioca, sugar, and salt and let stand. Line a pie tin with pastry and have ready pastry cut in strips for lattice top. Fresh or canned cherries, pitted and unsweetened, may be used. Combine fruit and juice mixture and pour in pie shell. Dot with butter, and top with pastry strips. Seal edges, building up a rim or binding with parchment pie tape— a special bit of equipment readily available from kitchen supply stores that helps prevent juice overflow and reduces edge darkening. Bake in a very hot oven (450°F) for 10 minutes, then 25 minutes in a moderate oven (350°F).

Black Walnut Cherry Pie

February 1939

2 c. pitted red cherries, unsweetened
1¼ cups cherry juice
1½ c. sugar
¼ tsp. cinnamon
1 envelope unflavored gelatin
½ c. cold water
½ c. black walnut meats
whipped cream
1 tsp. sugar
1 drop almond extract

Drain cherries, measure juice. Mix juice, sugar, and cinnamon and heat to boiling. Pour over gelatin which has been softened in cold water. Add cherries. Cool to soft jelly stage. Fold in nuts. Just before it congeals, pour into freshly baked pie shell and let stand until firm. Top with whipped cream, sweetened with 1 tsp. sugar, and flavored with almond extract. Sprinkle with a few nut meats.

Pineapple Pie

October 1929

⅓ c. milk
1 c. sugar
2 eggs, separated
½ c. cream
1 tbsp. butter
1 tbsp. flour
pinch of salt
1 c. crushed pineapple

Make a sauce of all ingredients except pineapple as for Butterscotch Pie I (page 118), saving egg whites for meringue. Add strained pineapple. Pour into baked crust. Add meringue (see page 123) and bake at 425°F till browned.

Raisin Meringue Pie

May 1929

2 eggs, separated
1 c. sour cream
¼ c. sugar
1 c. chopped raisins
1 c. chopped walnuts
¼ tsp. salt
1 tsp. vanilla
¼ c. powdered sugar for meringue

Beat egg yolks, then add sour cream, sugar, raisins, nuts, salt, and vanilla. Pour into a unbaked pastry-lined pie tin and bake in a moderate oven (350°F) for 30 minutes. Remove from oven, add meringue made from egg whites and powdered sugar, return to oven and bake slowly (300°F) for 15 minutes.

Lemon Pie

1934

Large (9-inch)
1½ c. sugar
few grains salt
7 tbsp. cornstarch
2 c. boiling water
3 egg yolks, beaten
⅓ c. + 1 tbsp. lemon juice
grated rind of 1 lemon
1½ tbsp. butter
meringue (see page 123; use 3 egg whites
and 6 tbsp. sugar)

Small (8-inch)
1 c. sugar
few grains salt
4½ tbsp. cornstarch
1⅓ c. boiling water
2 egg yolks, beaten
¼ c. lemon juice
grated rind of half lemon
1 tbsp. butter
meringue (see page 123)

Mix sugar, salt, and cornstarch together thoroughly in the top portion of a double-boiler; add boiling water slowly, cook until thickened, stirring constantly. Set over hot water in the bottom portion of the double boiler and cook 15 minutes. Add a little of mixture to beaten yolks, then add yolks to the sugar mixture and return to stove; cook 3 minutes. Remove, add lemon juice and rind and butter. Cool slightly, pour in baked shell. Cover with meringue, spreading clear to edges. Bake 20 minutes at 325°F. Let cool slowly and give time to set before serving.

Lemon Fluff Pie

May 1927

Tonight, serve the favorite of favorites...real *fresh*-lemon pie, with its golden filling...and topping of lightly-browned meringue! Just be sure to use plenty of Sunkist Lemon juice to give the tantalizing flavor that is all-important to success.

FREE BOOKLET OF 200 RECIPES

Seven different kinds of lemon pie, some with easy crumb crust, are described in Sunkist's colorful booklet of 200 recipes. Mail coupon.

Copr., 1936, California Fruit Growers Exchange

for dessert *tonight*

"I wonder how many readers bake lemon fluff pie. This is one of the many recipes I have found good. We were all delighted with it. I am giving this recipe together with a few of my own 'best sellers.'"

—*Mrs. C.A. Lyons, West Virginia*

Crust:
1½ c. flour
1 tsp. salt
½ c. shortening
½ tsp. baking powder
enough water to make soft dough

This will make 2 shells. I bake my shells on inverted pie pans. This way you will have a perfect shell. Bake 18 to 20 minutes at 425°F, or until lightly browned.

Filling:
3 eggs, separated
1 c. sugar
3 tbsp. cold water
grated rind and juice of 1 lemon
¼ tsp. salt

Beat yolks up with one-half of the sugar. Add water, lemon rind, and juice. Cook in double boiler until thick. Have eggs whites beaten stiff; add salt and remaining half cup of sugar. Pour into this the cooked mixture while hot, blending it well. Fill baked shell. Bake in slow oven (300°F), not above moderate, for 5 minutes. Brown lightly under broiler.

Lemon "Cake" Pie

July 1931

1 c. sugar
3 tbsp. flour
1/4 c. butter
3 eggs, separated
juice and grated rind of 1 lemon
2 c. milk

Mix sugar and flour and slightly softened butter. Add slightly beaten egg yolks, then lemon rind and juice and when well blended add milk. Fold in beaten egg whites and bake in unbaked rich crust in slow oven (325°F) about 40 minutes. Makes 2 8-inch pies with custard in bottom and sponge cake on top.

Grapefruit Pie

October 1930

4 tbsp. cornstarch
1¼ c. sugar
1¼ c. boiling water
1 tsp. butter
2 eggs, separated
1½ grapefruits, juiced
juice of ½ lemon
2 tbsp. confectioner's sugar
1 tsp. lemon juice

Mix cornstarch and sugar and add boiling water, stirring constantly. Cook until smooth and clear, add butter, slightly-beaten egg yolks, and strained fruit juices. Cool, pour into a baked shell, and cover with a meringue made of the stiffly-beaten egg whites, 2 tbsp. powdered sugar, and 1 tsp. lemon juice. Bake 15 minutes in a slow oven (300°F) until set and delicately browned.

—*Mrs. M.D., Wisconsin*

The woman who owns one will tell you—Write for booklet "What women say"

NESCO PERFECT
OIL COOK STOVE

❧ *Gooseberry Goodies* ❧

By Alice G. Hoffman, July 1928

Gooseberries are the backward children of the berry family. Like the modest, retiring members of the human clan, their virtues and latent possibilities are often overlooked.

So it seems only fair and just that someone should champion the cause of this down-trodden member of the berry family. So here and now we make a plea for the plain, retiring, and almost forgotten Mr. Goose Berry. He has many fine qualities. Our grandmothers, who knew him more intimately, were very fond of him. They knew how to get the most out of him, and found him very adaptable. Fortunately, they have left us records of some of their ways of dealing with him.

Gooseberry Pie

Stem and wash as many gooseberries as may be needed to fill the pie pans that you have filled with a rich pie pastry. (editor's note: Use 4 cups fresh, or 2 16-oz. cans gooseberries, drained, for 2 pies.) Fill the pans about ¾ full with the berries. Sugar well and add a top crust, being careful to pinch tightly around the edges to keep juice from boiling out. Bake in a hot oven (450°F) for 10 minutes, then reduce heat to 350°F. Serve plain or with whipped cream.

Pear Coronet Pie

April 1938

½ c. flour
⅔ c. sugar
1/8 tsp. salt
2 c. milk, scalded
2 tsp. butter
3 egg yolks
¾ tsp. vanilla
2 to 3 drops almond extract
6 to 8 canned pear halves, well drained
cherries, preserved ginger, or red jelly for garnish

Combine flour, sugar, and salt thoroughly in top of double boiler. Add scalded milk slowly, stirring well. Cook over hot water, stirring often, until mixture is thick and smooth; add butter. Beat egg yolks slightly; add a little hot mixture; stir quickly into filling. Stir and cook until eggs thicken. Remove from heat and cool. Add flavorings. Fill cooled baked pastry shell. Arrange pears, rounded end toward rim of pastry, pressing lightly so that surface of pears is flush with filling. Fill hollows of pears with whole or chopped cherries, chopped preserved ginger, bit of red jelly, etc. Fill space between pears and in center with meringue: 3 egg whites left-over from filling, beaten with sugar until stiff. Bake in a very slow oven (325°F) to brown the meringue.

Two Reader-Testers comment in this fashion: "I have rated this pie for special occasions, but my boys disagree with me and say it should be every day." "Whether I make the topping the same way or not, I shall always use [this] recipe for cream filling; [it] is perfect."

Rhubarb Pie I

April 1925

Follow recipe for Baked Rhubarb (below) and when cooked, place in a baked pie shell and serve hot.

Baked Rhubarb:
3 c. diced and scalded rhubarb
1 c. sugar
⅛ tsp. salt
1 tsp. cinnamon
1 tbsp. butter

Mix rhubarb, sugar, and salt; sprinkle with cinnamon and dot with butter. Place in uncovered baking dish and cook slowly (300°F) until rhubarb is tender and some of the juice has evaporated.

Variation:
Add ½ c. raisins to 2 c. rhubarb and proceed as above.

Rhubarb Pie II

April 1925

3 c. rhubarb
1 c. sugar
⅛ tsp. salt
2 tbsp. flour

Mix thoroughly, place between unbaked crusts, bake in a quick oven (450°F) for 15 minutes, then reduce the heat of the oven to 350°F for remaining 15 minutes to keep the juice from boiling over.

Rhubarb Custard Pie

May 1931

1 c. rhubarb
1 c. sugar
2 tbsp. flour
1 c. sweet milk
2 eggs, separated
pinch salt

Cook rhubarb with ½ c. of sugar in saucepan. Mix rest of sugar and flour. Add hot milk and cook until thick in top of double boiler. Beat egg yolks and stir in. Add rhubarb and salt and continue to cook until thick in consistency. Allow to cool. Fill baked pastry shell and cover with meringue (see page 123) made with reserved egg whites. Brown in slow oven (300°F).

—*Mrs. B. W., Missouri*

Raspberry Pie

May 1910

Put a pint of berries in a granite saucepan, add 2 tbsp. water and 3 tbsp. of sugar and shake over the fire until the juice flows freely, but do not let the berries lose their shape. Skim them out and boil the syrup until clear. Cream together butter the size of an egg with 1 tbsp. of powdered sugar, add 1 tbsp. fine breadcrumbs, a few drops of almond flavoring, and the well-beaten yolks of 2 eggs. Lastly stir in the whites, whipped stiff. Line plates with a nice unbaked pastry and spread with the raspberries, pour over them the syrup, and spread with the egg mixture. Bake in a hot oven (400°F) until baked through.

"WELL! WHERE DID YOU GET THAT IDEA?"

"DOESN'T IT LOOK GOOD? THE RECIPE WAS IN MY PILLSBURY'S BEST BAG!"

SKILLET PEACH COBBLER

. . . proves what good things you can make for very little money with a good recipe and a good flour!

THE "GOOD RECIPE" IS IN YOUR BAG OF PILLSBURY'S BEST — AND SO IS THE "GOOD FLOUR"!

"Better things to eat for less money" — that's the reason Pillsbury's Best is in the pantries of millions of women who are known to their friends and neighbors as good cooks.

In every bag of Pillsbury's Best there is a recipe folder — and the recipes are the kind that every woman wants! They're practical and inexpensive

—yet they make unusual, attractive, delicious foods. And the flour itself means better baking for less money! Pillsbury's Best is a "balanced" flour, made from a special blend of wheats, to eliminate the seasonal changes in quality found in a flour made from only one wheat. As a result, Pillsbury's Best works perfectly for all kinds of baking—and it never causes an expensive, wasteful baking failure.

Pillsbury's Best Flour may cost a little more per sack — *but in the long run it costs less per baking.* And it's a real pleasure to use it — Pillsbury's Best is so fine, so good, so dependable.

PILLSBURY'S BEST . . . *the "balanced" flour*

Peach Custard Pie

November 1911

Fill the unbaked crust with sliced peaches, pour in an ordinary custard mixture—1 c. milk cooked thick with ½ c. + 1 tbsp. sugar and 2 tbsp. flour, 2 egg yolks beaten in slowly, then the mixture cooled—and bake slowly (325°F) until the custard sets.

— *Mrs. Whitehouse*

Berry-Banana Crumb Pie

June 1936

12 graham crackers
⅓ c. softened butter
¼ c. + 1 tbsp. sugar
1 c. fresh strawberries
1 c. sliced bananas
sweetened whipped cream

Roll crackers, mix with butter and ¼ c. sugar. Press firmly in a buttered pie tin, reserving a few crumbs. Bake 15 minutes in a moderately hot oven (400°F), cool, and when ready to serve, fill with berries mixed with 1 tbsp. sugar and bananas. Spread cream over top, sprinkle with remaining crumbs.

—*Mrs. C.W., California*

❧ *Gentlemen Prefer Pies* ❧

By Sarah Gibbs Campbell, December 1933

A short while ago I discovered some very old cook books in which I found several recipes for unusual pies. They sounded almost too good to be true, but when I tried them my family agreed with me that they were not only good but "the best ever."

[U]ntil I saw the popularity of my new pies among the masculine members of my family, I had never realized how much "gentlemen prefer pies." In nine cases out of ten, pie was placed at the head of a long list of popular desserts; fruit pie, custard pie, mince pie, coconut pie, chiffon and meringue pie, young or old, every man has his favorite.

Grapefruit Chiffon Pie is delicate and appetizing; substitute grated pineapple and the result is wonderful, and for lovers of coconut, Orange-Coconut Pie leaves little to be desired. Quince Cream Pie has the flavor and aroma of by-gone days when grandmother made quince preserves and makes us wonder why we so seldom see quince trees anymore. Cheese-Lemon Pie is made by the "best cook" of a little Mennonite village and is a whole meal in itself.

Pineapple Chiffon Pie

4 eggs, separated
1 c. sugar
½ c. grated pineapple
1 tbsp. lemon juice
2 tbsp. powdered sugar

Beat the egg yolks and sugar together, beat until very light. Add slowly to the pineapple which has been heated in a double boiler. Add the lemon juice and cook until thick, beating all the time. Beat the whites until very stiff, fold half into the yolk and fruit mixture, which has been cooled slightly. Cut and fold the sifted powdered sugar into the remaining whites. Pour filling into a baked pastry shell, cover with meringue (which you made with your whites and sugar) and bake in a very moderate oven (300°F) until delicately browned.

Variations:

Grapefruit Chiffon Pie

In the above recipe, substitute 1/3 c. grapefruit juice for the pineapple and lemon juice. Follow mixing and baking directions for Pineapple Chiffon Pie. This is a very dainty pie.

Orange-Coconut Pie

⅓ c. orange juice

1 c. shredded unsweetened coconut

4 eggs, separated

1 c. sugar

Follow the directions for Pineapple Chiffon Pie, but substitute orange juice for pineapple and lemon juice. Then fold in all the egg whites, pour into a baked shell and sprinkle the coconut over the top. Bake in a very moderate oven (300°F) until the filling is set and the coconut delicately toasted.

Quince Cream Pie

3 eggs, separated

¾ c. sugar

½ c. thick cream

1 c. strained cooked quince

1 tbsp. lemon juice

2 tbsp. powdered sugar

Beat the egg yolks and sugar together, stir in the cream, then the quince and lemon juice. Cook in a double boiler until thick, then fold in 1 stiffly beaten egg white. Pour into a baked shell, cover with a meringue made of the remaining whites and the powdered sugar. Bake in a very moderate oven (300°F) between 10 and 15 minutes; the filling should be set and the meringue browned.

Cheese-Lemon Pie

2 c. cottage or cream cheese

¼ c. rich cream

1 c. sugar

3 tbsp. lemon juice

grated rind of 1 lemon

4 eggs, separated

Mash the cheese fine and mix it with the cream, sugar, lemon juice, and rind. Add the yolks one at a time, beating well. Beat the whites until very stiff, then cut and fold into the cheese mixture. Pour into a deep pan lined with unbaked pastry and bake in a hot oven (400°F) for 10 or 15 minutes, then reduce the heat to moderate (350°F) and bake until the filling is set and the top very delicately browned.

Holiday Pies

❧ Thanksgiving Reminders ❧

By Mabel K. Ray, November 1933

Among other good things fall ushers in is the 2.And I like mine not too dark, please—nor too spicy! Perhaps you'll like it, too. The pumpkin is cut into small squares and steamed or boiled until tender, then run through a sieve (editor's note: or the food processor). Return pumpkin to the stove and cook it slowly until the water does not separate out. Then make filling as follows:

3 c. strained pumpkin
3 eggs
⅔ c. sugar (granulated or light brown)
1 pt. milk
½ tsp. ginger
½ tsp. cinnamon
2 tbsp. flour

Add slightly beaten eggs to strained pumpkin, then add sugar, milk, and seasonings. Stir flour over mixture and combine. Pour into unbaked pie shell and bake at 350°F for 1 hour. Makes 1 large or 2 medium pies.

Individual Pumpkin Pie

November 1921

⅔ c. brown sugar
½ c. steamed and strained pumpkin
2½ c. milk
2 eggs
1 tsp. cinnamon
½ tsp. ground ginger
½ tsp. salt
1 tsp. grated lemon peel

Mix the ingredients and turn into individual unbaked pie shells—between 4½ and 5 inches around, readily available at bakers' supply shops. Bake in a slow oven (275°F to 300°F) and when cold serve with whipped cream. Will make about 6 small pies.

to Satisfy that
Healthy Appetite

To preserve the rich, natural flavor of pumpkins, apples, cranberries, or any of the delicious fall fruits, be sure to cook them in glassy-surfaced, food-acid-resisting Nesco Royal Granite Enameled Ware. The preserving kettle and the saucepan, in any size, are handy utensils for such use.

Crisp Autumn days! Sharp appetites! Father, Mother, children—all are eager for good, hearty meals these glorious days. Make the preparing easier for mother and the girls, by using famous Nesco Royal Granite Enameled Ware—the durable ware.

Cooking is easy and economical, be-cause this famous ware conserves heat. Cooking is safe, because the glassy, glossy enamel surface resists food acids and impairment of flavor. Cleaning, after the meal is over, is made easier, because of the smooth enamel surface. A kitchen furnished in this beautiful blue-grey ware is indeed a joy and pride.

Famous Nesco Royal Granite Enameled Ware, in all sizes and styles of utensils, is sold at popular prices at leading hard-ware, housefurnishing, and general stores.

To introduce the famous ware into your home we'll send you this handy little sauce pan, if you'll send us your dealer's name and a dime to cover postage and packing.

Address: National Enameling & Stamping Co., Inc.
Advertising Department, Section F, Milwaukee, Wis.

NATIONAL ENAMELING & STAMPING CO., Inc.
St. Louis   Granite City, Ill.   New York   Milwaukee
Baltimore   Chicago   New Orleans   Philadelphia

NESCO ROYAL GRANITE ENAMELED WARE

❧ Pie That Is Pie ❧

November 1931

Of all pies—pumpkin still seems to retain first place for Thanksgiving. And it certainly isn't any wonder when it's so spicy and full of flavor. A meringue of whipped cream sprinkled with chopped nuts added just before it is served gives a different touch liked by many.

Pumpkin Pie with Black Walnut Crust

November 1936

1½ c. rich milk
2¼ c. cooked, strained pumpkin or squash
1 c. brown sugar
1½ tsp. cinnamon
⅛ tsp. cloves
½ tsp. nutmeg
½ tsp. ginger
¾ tsp. salt
3 eggs

Truly delicious is this simple variation of pumpkin pie. Use a good, rich pastry recipe (such as Plain Pastry—2-Crusts, page 110) and blend the flour, salt, and shortening for the crust as usual. For each crust add 2 tbsp. finely chopped black walnuts. Add water as usual and roll. Line a deep pie tin with this crust and chill thoroughly.

Scald milk. Mix pumpkin, sugar, spices, and salt. Add eggs, slightly beaten, and scalded milk. Mix well.

GRANDMA'S
PUNKIN PIE

Pour into the chilled unbaked crust and sprinkle top with a few fairly large nut meats before baking. Put at once in a hot oven (425°F to 450°F). Bake 10 minutes at this temperature, reduce heat to moderate (325°F to 350°F) and bake until set, about 30 minutes. This keeps the under crust crisp and inviting yet the filling is just right.

Sweet Potato Pie

February 1910

Make a custard of 1 pt. milk, 3 eggs, and ½ c. sugar. Beat yolks until light, add milk and sugar. Press the sweet potatoes (editor's note: about 1 to 2 medium to large sweet potatoes, enough to yield 1 c.) which have been peeled and steamed through a sieve, and stir into milk and eggs. Season with cinnamon and 1 tbsp. melted butter. Put in unbaked crust before baking at 350°F. When done, make a meringue out of the whites of eggs, spread over the top of the pie, and return to oven to brown.

Colonial Innkeepers Pecan Pie

March 1938

3 eggs
½ c. sugar
¼ tsp. salt
1 tsp. vanilla
1 c. dark corn syrup
1 c. melted butter
1 c. whole pecan meats

Beat eggs, add sugar, salt, and vanilla and beat lightly. Add syrup and butter. Place pecans in bottom of unbaked crust, add filling. Bake in moderate oven (350°F) for 50 to 60 minutes.

Cranberry Molasses Pie

November 1929

1 qt. ripe cranberries
1 c. brown sugar
1 tbsp. butter
1 c. white sugar
1 c. molasses

Cook ingredients over a slow fire for 10 minutes.

Line a deep pie dish with piecrust. Fill with cranberry mixture. Cover with strips of crust, criss-cross. Bake in a slow oven (300°F) for 45 minutes to 1 hour, or until the berries are thoroughly cooked.

Tarts

TARTS Rhyme with HEARTS

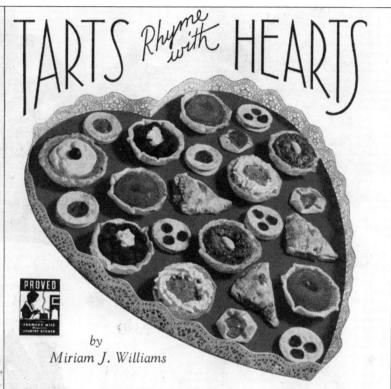

by
Miriam J. Williams

THERE'S a twinge at the heartstrings when we are asked to think back upon tarts "like Mother used to make."

But how different are the tarts we recall as our favorites. One friend says that they must be two-layered rounds of pastry, toothsome, and flaky, with a fair-sized hole in the top layer for jelly to "squash" (that's her word) through. . . . . . Something like that, declares another, but there must be at least three small holes, cut with a thimble,—Mother's old thimble with a needle hole worn in the top. . . . . Well, *my* mother's tarts in New England were three-cornered, fat, brown tarts with a filling that tasted like more, and so on.

The result of these many descriptions of tarts was that the Country Kitchen tried them all and arranged them on a big heart-shaped tray, described later.

To make the tarts, start with flaky pastry, yet not so tender that it crumbles with necessary handling. Make tart shells by shaping pastry rounds over muffin tins (we used 4½ inch ones for our tins). After rounds are cut, prick them all over with a fork, then shape to the outside of the tin by pinching in six or seven tucks, giving the tart a fluted edge. Or line a small tart tin with pastry, and prick well before baking. If they insist on puffing inside, fill center with rice before baking.

There's no limit to the variety of fillings. A famous tea-room tart is made with a spoonful of luscious cream-pie filling in the bottom, then fresh or canned or preserved fruit, drained of juice. Then the tarts are topped with a beautiful transparent glaze which makes them a sight not soon forgotten. Or whipped cream may be used.

Not always is a topping necessary, as in those cinnamon apple tarts pictured, where a half of a blushing apple and its syrup glaze, cooked almost to the jelly stage, was too attractive to hide with whipped cream.

Country Kitchen Recipes for Tarts

Banbury Tarts

2 tblsp. butter
¼ c. sugar
1 egg
¼ c. candied fruit peel
½ c. raisins or currants
2 tblsp. cookie crumbs
Dash of nutmeg and cinnamon

Cream butter, add sugar, egg, and mix well. Add other ingredients. Put a spoonful on one side of a 6-inch round or square of pastry, rolled thin. Fold over, crimp edges. Brush top with beaten egg mixed with a little cream and sugar. Bake in a hot oven (400° F.) about 15 minutes or until brown. Makes 8 tarts.

Lemon Butter

6 eggs
1 lb. (2¼ c.) sugar
¼ lb. (½ c.) butter
3 large lemons, juice
Grated rind of 2 lemons
Sprinkle salt

Beat eggs in top of double boiler. Add other ingredients. Cook over hot water, stirring constantly, until thick. Cool, store in glass jar in cool place. This keeps indefinitely, serving as filling for fresh cake or pudding sauce. It is not stiff enough to cut for a pie filling but makes delicious tarts when put in baked tart shells, topped with whipped cream or meringue and a preserved strawberry. —*Mrs. D. H. B., Tennessee.*

Cheese Pies

1½ c. cottage cheese
⅔ c. cream
⅓ c. honey
2 tblsp. sugar
1 tblsp. cornstarch
Sprinkle salt
Grated rind of orange
3 eggs, separated
8 pastry-lined tins

Run cheese through a fine sieve, add cream, honey, cornstarch mixed with sugar, salt, and beaten egg yolks. Fold in stiffly beaten whites. Bake in pastry lined tins, first in a hot oven (425° F.) then in moderate oven until set.

Pecan Tarts

3 eggs
1 c. sugar
1 c. corn syrup
Dash salt
¾ c. pecan nut meats, coarsely chopped
1 tsp. vanilla
8 pastry-lined tins

Beat eggs slightly, add other ingredients. Pour into tins lined with pastry. Rather shallow, small muffin tins are best, since the filling is very rich. Bake in a very moderate oven (350° F.) about 40 minutes or until a knife blade thrust in the center comes out clean. Loosen from the pans before entirely cold.

Continued on Page 41

Apple Tart

February 1937

Pastry-lined tin (see recipe for Lemon Tart Crust, page 156)
4 apples
3 tbsp. flour mixed with 2 tbsp. sugar
½ c. sugar mixed with cinnamon
butter
3 tbsp. water

Peel and core apples. Halve lengthwise, from stem to blossom end. In the bottom of the pastry-lined tin, sprinkle sugar and flour. Put in apples, round side up. Sprinkle sugar and cinnamon over top, dot with butter. Pour in water and put in a moderately hot oven (375°F to 400°F). Bake until apples are soft, about 40 minutes. As soon as removed from the oven, pour in about ¼ c. boiling water, shaking until it is absorbed. Serve slightly warm, plain or with ice cream or whipped cream as a special treat.

Cranberry Meringue Tarts

February 1937

1 c. ground cranberries
2 egg yolks
¾ c. sugar
sprinkle salt
½ envelope unflavored gelatin
2 tbsp. cold water
2 egg whites
4 tbsp. sugar
8 baked tartlet shells (see recipe for Lemon Tart Crust, page 156)

Run raw cranberries through a food chopper to make a cupful. Combine cranberries, beaten egg yolks, sugar, and salt. Cook over slow fire until thickened slightly. Remove, add gelatin soaked in cold water and stir. Chill. When fairly thick, fold in whites beaten until stiff with 4 tbsp. sugar added gradually. Pile in baked tartlet shells and chill. Top with whipped cream.

Gooseberry Tart

July 1928

Wash and pick over the berries. Stew them in as little water as possible. When their skins burst, remove from the fire and rub through a colander, or put through a fruit press. (editor's note: Contemporary readers will likely use canned gooseberries, which can be run through the blender or food processor. Use one 16-oz. can, drained, per tart.) Sweeten to taste and pour into shallow pie-pans [or tart pans] filled with rich unbaked pastry (see recipe for Lemon Tart Crust, page 156). Put pastry strips, lattice-fashion, over the top and bake in a moderate oven (350°F).

Marlboro Tart

March 1924

2 eggs
2 c. grated apple
½ lemon, juice and grated rind
1 c. sugar
2 tbsp. melted butter
1 c. seeded raisins
pastry (See recipe for Lemon Tart Crust, page 156)

Beat eggs, add remaining ingredients and turn into an unbaked pastry-lined pie dish. Cover the top with strips of pastry arranged lattice fashion and finish with a strip of pastry around the edge. Place in hot oven (400°F), reducing heat after 15 minutes to 350°F. Bake until firm in the center.

156

Plum Tartlets

July 1929

Line tins, or paper baking cups, with store-bought puff pastry, following package directions for thawing. Stew a sufficient quantity of choice ripe plums with an ample amount of sugar and a bit of water until cooked tender. Fill each pastry shell with this and bake in a quick oven (450°F). As soon as pastry is puffed and nicely golden, remove them from the oven, serving them either hot or cold—but always freshly baked—with whipped cream sprinkled liberally with shredded cocoanut. Plum preserves make desirable filling for these tartlets.

Lemon Tart

February 1937

Filling:
6 tbsp. flour
2 c. sugar
2 c. milk
2 lemons, juice and grated rind
2 eggs, lightly beaten

Crust:
3½ c. sifted flour
½ tsp. baking soda
½ tsp. salt
1 c. sugar
¼ c. butter and lard
⅔ to ¾ c. buttermilk

For filling, mix flour, sugar, and milk together and cook in a saucepan until thick and smooth. Add lemon juice and rind and pour over eggs. Cool slightly. Mix crust by sifting together dry ingredients. Work in fat as for pie crust, add milk to make a soft dough. Roll out, making 2 rounds and extra for top strips. Fit rounds into 2 small pie tins. Put half of filling in each, lay strips, 3 inches wide, across the top. Bake in a hot oven (400°F) until brown.

A GOOD REFRIGERATOR SAVES
TIME, HEALTH, STRENGTH, MONEY

by Bess M. Rowe

Photographs: Elec-
trolux; Frigidaire;
General Electric;
Kelvinator; Norge;
Superfex; and West-
inghouse

HAVING a good refrigerator does not always mean getting the best service from it, say the experts on refrigeration, so we consulted several of them and now bring you, from them,

A Fourteen-Point Program for Good Refrigeration

1. *Size.* All who have studied refrigeration say, "Buy the largest size refrigerator you can afford." A family of four or five needs a refrigerator of 6 to 8 cubic feet capacity, leaning toward the larger rather than the smaller size.

To check this advice we asked members of our Reader Test Group to keep a record of the contents of their refrigerators for one week. The reports came from 25 states. They give a good cross section of the refrigeration demands in farm homes. The average amount of milk stored, according to these records, is 4.3 quarts; of cream, 3.6 pints, or more than seven of the half-pint bottles usually found in town and city refrigerators. Butter averages 2.18 pounds. Dough is stored in refrigerators some time during the week—a new development in home baking. There were few women who didn't have dressed chickens in the refrigerator at least once during the week—eight in one case.

There was a wide range in other meats stored. One homemaker started the week with 50 pounds; one reported half of a freshly killed lamb; another, a whole boiled ham; another, 50 pounds of sausage.

Fruit juices and fruits for cold drinks ran high. Planning meals to avoid heating up the kitchens put a large number of cooked foods into refrigerators, ready for quick reheating. Three to five kinds of cooked vegetables were not unusual.

When you add salad dressing, sandwich spread, cheese, and cottage cheese, berries, peaches, pears and melons and other fresh fruits, eggs, peanut butter and yeast, you realize why "the largest refrigerator you possibly can afford" is a good rule.

2. *Where To Put the Refrigerator.* It is better, as a rule, to place the refrigerator near the door where food is brought into the kitchen. In any case, it should be easily accessible, so that your kitchen "mileage" will not mount up in a day's work.

For economical service, a refrigerator must have "room to breathe." If cupboards are built around it, there should be some eight inches of free space above the refrigerator. Two or three inches at sides and back are none too much for circulation of air. Without this spacing, your fuel bill will be larger.

With an ice box, it is much more convenient to install a permanent drain—the drain pan is sure to be forgotten occasionally, even in the best of families!

3. *Care of a Refrigerator.* A new refrigerator should be cleaned before it is chilled. Some experts advise washing the cooling trays and shelves with hot water, and soap; the food compartment, with warm water, to which soda or borax has

Good Food Arrangement: Above—Automatic Refrigerator; Upper Right—Top Icing Icebox

been added. Non-abrasive cleaners also are good for cleaning.

A tablespoonful of sal soda sprinkled on the cake of ice once a week, is recommended for an icebox.

4. *Defrosting and Icing.* Defrost an automatic refrigerator when the frost is one-fourth inch thick, or when it looks glazed—or defrost and clean once a week.

5. *Keep the Air Circulating.* The cooling value of either an automatic refrigerator or an icebox is cut down by any interference with the circulation of air inside the box. Wrapping food in paper or paper bags not only cuts off the cold air from the food inside, but the packages are apt

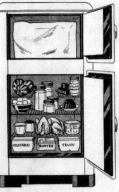

to be crowded together and the circulation of air cut down.

Wrapping paper around the ice in an icebox seriously lessens its refrigerating value because it interferes with the circulation of air. Also, the ice chamber is for ice, *not* for food!

Another practice which cuts down refrigerating value, is to put paper on the shelves.

6. *Avoid Crowding.* Sides of dishes should not be against the side or back of the food chamber, nor should the dishes be placed too close together. Many kinds of covered dishes are made especially for

Continued on Page 28

Other Pastries

Cream Puffs

March 1931

1 c. boiling water
½ c. butter
1 c. flour
4 eggs

Heat the water and butter in a sauce pan until the water boils, then add the flour all at once and stir vigorously. Cook over the fire until the mass is thick and smooth. When it is thick enough it will ball up on the spoon. Remove from fire when it has reached this stage and add the eggs, unbeaten, one at a time. Drop by spoonfuls on an oiled baking sheet. Bake in a moderate oven (350°F), from 25 to 30 minutes. When puffs are cool, make an incision in the side and fill with cream filling or whipped cream.

Cream Filling:
¾ c. sugar
½ c. flour
⅛ tsp. salt
2 c. milk
1 square unsweetened chocolate, melted
2 eggs
1 tsp. vanilla

Mix sugar, flour, and salt together. Add milk, which has been heated. Boil, add melted chocolate if desired, add slightly beaten eggs and cook for a few minutes in top of double boiler. Cool and flavor with vanilla.

Whipped Cream Filling for Cream Puffs:
A filling of flavored and sweetened whipped cream may be used in the cream puffs if desired.

Southern Apple Dumplings

October 1938

Dumplings:
2 c. flour
2 tsp. baking powder
½ tsp. salt
2 tbsp. butter
¾ c. milk
1 c. chopped, peeled apple
2 tsp. lemon juice (not if apples are tart)

Sift flour, measure and resift with baking powder and salt into mixing bowl. Work in butter with finger tips; when well-blended, add milk and stir vigorously until dry ingredients are wet. Turn out on floured board, knead very slightly to make dough smooth, and roll out to ¼ inch thickness. Cut in 6 to 8 squares and in the center of each piece place 2 to 3 tbsp. of chopped apple, moistened with lemon juice. Wet edges of dough and pinch together around apple. Drop dumplings, seam side down, into boiling hot sauce made as follows:

Sauce:
2 c. white sugar
½ c. brown sugar
2 tbsp. flour
½ tsp. salt
dash nutmeg, if desired
2 c. water
½ c. butter

Mix dry ingredients in deep skillet or baking pan (about 10 inches in diameter), add water and butter, and cook with constant stirring until thick. When dumplings are added, cover and place in a hot oven (425°F) for 30 minutes. Then remove cover, baste dumplings with sauce, and continue cooking uncovered until dumplings are golden brown. Serve with sauce and a scoop of vanilla ice cream.

Rhubarb Dumplings
April 1925

2 c. flour
4 tsp. baking powder
½ tsp. salt
2 tbsp. lard or butter
¾ c. milk
2 c. diced and scalded rhubarb
1½ c. sugar
2 c. water

Mix flour, baking powder, and salt. Cut in shortening as for biscuit. Add milk and mix lightly into a soft dough. Divide into 6 equal parts and roll each into a circle ½ inch thick. Mix rhubarb and ½ c. sugar and pile uncooked in equal parts of the 6 circles of dough. Bring water and 1 c. sugar to a boil. Bring up edges of dough around rhubarb, pinching it in place. Lay with smooth side up in the boiling syrup. Bake in hot oven (450°F) approximately 25 to 30 minutes; the dumplings are done when the pastry is golden.

Cherry Turnovers
June 1910

Rub 1 c. butter into 1 lb. flour. When like coarse meal, moisten with 1 c. or less ice water and work to a paste, handling as little as possible. Roll out on a floured board, fold up and roll for the second and third time, if still very cold, use at once, if not, set in the ice box until chilled. Roll out and cut into rounds the size of large biscuits. Drain juice off sweetened canned or freshly stewed stoned cherries and chop. Mix with 2 well beaten eggs, and a little lemon juice, put 1 tbsp. of the cherry mixture on ½ each round of the crust, fold other half over and pinch edges together. Lay these half-circles on a floured or buttered tin and bake to a golden brown at 375°F. Sift sugar over them and serve either hot or cold.

Yeast Breads, Rolls, and Cakes

"I made it *all myself*"

Milk Bread

❧ A Loaf of Bread ❧

By Emma Thomas Scoville, March 1934

I like to make a loaf of bread,
For when I handle snowy flour
My thoughts go back to early Spring,
The sunshine and the silver shower.

And I can see the barren fields—
The farmer tilling moist brown earth,
The seeding and the sprouting time
And then the tiny green blades birth.

I see the tall stalk's bearded plumes
That ripple as they nod and sway.
Glad harvest time, rich golden wheat
A clacking mill—then flour today.

My heart is filled with gratitude:
That dear ones daily may be fed.
God left this lovely task for me
To make a fragrant loaf of bread.

Breads

Whole Wheat or Cracked Wheat Bread
1934

1 qt. milk
⅓ c. brown sugar or honey
6 tbsp. butter
2 tbsp. salt
2 cakes compressed yeast (editor's note: substitute
2 packages active dry yeast)
¼ c. lukewarm water
3 c. white flour and 6 c. whole-wheat flour
     -or-
4 c. white flour and 4 to 5 c. coarser wheat flour

Scald milk in a double boiler with sugar, butter, and salt. Cool to lukewarm. In a large bowl, soak yeast in water and add milk. Add enough whole-wheat flour to make a batter. Beat thoroughly; add rest of whole-wheat and white flour to knead. The dough should be of a softer consistency than for white bread but not actually sticky. Knead for 10 to 15 minutes; put into a greased bowl; cover; let rise at a temperature of 80°F to 85°F until double in bulk. Knead down slightly without adding more flour; cover; let rise again until double. Make into loaves and put in well-greased individual bread pans. Brush top with melted fat. Cover and let rise until double in bulk. Bake until a golden brown in a moderately hot oven (400°F). Yield: three loaves of 1¾ lbs. each before baking.

Bread—what home of hard-working people can do without it even to three times daily? Great variety is possible with a little alteration of foundation recipes. Mastery of good standard recipes . . . will open the door to an endless variety, and establish a firm reputation for good cooking.

A Man Makes Bread

in the
FARMER'S WIFE COUNTRY KITCHEN

George McKee

by Miriam Williams

1. Blend lukewarm milk or water, softened fat, sugar and salt. Add a pint or so of flour and stir enough to make a batter. (Avoid adding yeast along with fat, or some of the yeast plants will be coated with fat, and thus put out of action.) Then add the yeast, softened in lukewarm water. If flour and room are cold, milk can be slightly warmer. Use cooler liquid on a warm day.

2. After the rest of the flour is added in a cup or scoopfuls (don't beat in a little at a time for that makes a rubbery dough), turn the dough onto the board, kneading in any flour left in the bowl. A fairly stiff dough handles better, is not so subject to variations in temperature or handling as is a thin dough. The easy way is often the best way, so avoid over-beating.

3. The easy way, the no-knead method, makes a very acceptable loaf. Merely fold the dough over several times, let it rest 10 minute, then work lightly for ½ minute. Soft wheat flours respond well to this method. For the regular kneading method, knead the dough lightly for 6 to 8 minutes. This develops gluten, making finer textured bread.

4. The less familiar "breaking" method may be used for show loaves, as for exhibit, since it develops a fine silky texture and increases volume. Tear off bits of dough until the whole mass is separated, then mix together and repeat, for a total of 4 or 5 minutes. This gives a fine textured loaf.

5. Grease top, cover and let the dough rise in a warm place until double in bulk. Then give it a punch and about four folds and let rise again. This second rising may be omitted if time is short. Better 2 short risings than 1 over-long one, however.

6. To make bread into loaves, spank it out after the second rising. Cut off pieces for each loaf, tuck each piece in to make a ball. Let rest for 20 minutes in a warm room on the board, covering the dough with the bread pans to prevent a crust if the air is dry. Then the dough will flatten out and can be stretched into a long piece. Fold in the ends and sides neatly, roll to make a neat shaped loaf. Put in pans to rise.

7. For Parkerhouse rolls, let the balls of dough rest 10 to 15 minutes, smack with the side of the hand to make a crease, spread with fat, fold over, flatten down, put in pans to rise.

WHEN experienced farm women go home singing the praises of a man breadmaker you know that he's either charmed them into *thinking* that he knows his doughs, or that he really does know them.

There are very few men in the world who could be called experts at breadmaking, but after watching Mr. George McKee, of a famous yeast company, at work in our Country Kitchen for a day I'm convinced that he is one of them.

Using a new packaged quick yeast he turned out beautiful rolls and bread. He is technically accurate, skillful, and makes breadmaking easy. From many years' experience as a professional bread demonstrator he knows where trouble is likely to lurk for the experienced cook as well as for the beginner.

Now I know why women go a second and third time to his demonstrations and why they say with gratitude: "Now—at last—I'm making good bread." We recommend that you, too, try his recipe and method. And success to you in supplying your family with fragrant, golden brown loaves and pans of crusty rolls!

Recipe for 4 loaves

1 packet quick yeast	4 tsp. salt
1 c. lukewarm water	4 tsp. sugar
3 c. lukewarm milk,	4 tblsp. fat
or part water and	About 12 c. flour
part milk	

Soften yeast in lukewarm water. In a big bowl put the rest of the liquid (if raw milk is used, scald and cool to lukewarm), salt, sugar, and softened fat, cutting it into small pieces with the spoon. Add about a pint of flour, blend into a batter. Add yeast, then rest of flour, stirring it in

quickly with a spoon. Turn onto a floured board and knead lightly until smooth, about 7 or 8 minutes. For the no-knead method, fold the dough over several times, let rest 10 minutes, then work ½ minute. Cover and let rise in a greased bowl until nearly double in bulk (requires about 2 hours in a warm place). Turn onto board, flatten and fold over 4 times. Again let rise until nearly double in bulk (about 40 minutes). Turn onto board, cut into 4 pieces, fold into balls. Let rest 20 minutes, covered by bowl or pans. Flatten out, stretch, fold and roll into loaves. Grease top of loaves, let rise until nearly doubled, bake 45 to 50 minutes in a moderately hot oven (400° F.).

McKee-isms

"WOMEN seem to like the no-knead method. Everything's got to be less work now-a-days. That's all right by the men, just so they keep making home-made bread.

"Salt in bread is more important than folks think—it's one of the four indispensables: liquid, yeast, salt and flour. Salt keeps down the development of wild yeast, adds whiteness and strength.

"Golden brown crust is due to caramelization of sugar. If bread dough rises too long, so much of the sugar is turned into CO_2 gas by action of the yeast that there is none left by baking time. Result: the crust is a sickly pale color.

"Milk sugar is not converted by yeast action, so milk bread is likely to bake a better brown. Milk bread has higher food value, better flavor, better keeping quality than an all-water bread.

"Shortening acts as an internal lubricant. It softens gluten strands and adds richness in flavor.

Continued on Page 27

❧ Yeast: A Starter ❧

By Mrs. C.K.T., July 1913

Without good yeast it is impossible to have good bread. To begin with, obtain a package of good yeast, or better still a cup of sponge from a neighbor. Set your bread by using flour and warm water. When light and foamy, and ready to mix up, take out into a glass jar, a half teacupful. Stir into this a heaping teaspoonful of sugar. Set away in a cool place, but do not allow to freeze. At noon, previous to the next baking day, add to the contents of the jar a tablespoon of flour, and a little more sugar, and a half cup of water, stir well and set in a warm place.

This is your starter, which you will use in mixing your sponge at night. In the morning, save out a small portion of the sponge, as before and don't neglect to stir into it a little sugar but no salt.

Proceed in this way each time, adding a fresh cake of yeast to the sponge, say once in about every six weeks. The result will be very satisfactory.

Hot Cross Buns

March 1910

Take a bowl of bread dough after the first kneading. Set it aside to rise like the other bread dough; when light, knead into it ½ c. currants that have been washed and dried, ½ c. sugar, and nutmeg to flavor. Knead no more than is necessary to mix the ingredients. Form into round biscuits, and place in a baking pan about ½ inch apart. Cut 2 deep gashes on top of each, crossing each other, and set to rise in a warm place. Just before putting into the moderately hot oven (400°F), brush the tops with melted butter or white of egg. Bake 10 minutes then reduce heat to 350°F and bake about 15 minutes more, until golden.

PUT YOUR EQUIPMENT TO WORK . . . .

PROVED

The Country Kitchen finds it helpful to
USE A RING MOLD FOR—

- Coffee cake or pecan roll
- Upside-down cake; fruit cake
- Steamed pudding or ice-box pudding
- Chilled potato salad garnished with quartered tomatoes and deviled egg halves

- Meat, chicken or fish loaf with creamed vegetables
- Noodle, macaroni or rice ring with creamed meat or chicken
- Vegetable souffle with cheese or bacon sauce
- Jellied salad or dessert

For baked things, first grease or oil the mold thoroughly. For jellied dishes, first rinse in cold water and to unmold, set in lukewarm water a few minutes. Turn ring mold out on chop plate or platter. Garnish appropriately, serve at the table. Just the thing for club luncheons or guest dinners.

❧ *Wheat for the World!* ❧
These Women Are for Patriotic Women, Determined
to be Wheat-Savers for Humanity's Sake

September 1917

In time of war as in time of peace it is not only important, but essential, that people be well fed. Victory does not depend alone on guns and soldiers; it depends as well on the efficiency of every man, woman and child back of the firing line. To maintain this efficiency there must be enough food and it must be so cooked and so combined as to be both palatable and nourishing . . .

The war must be won in the kitchens and on the dining tables of America as well as in the trenches. The Department of Agriculture stands ready to supply information to help the housewife do her bit toward winning this war.

—Carl Vrooman, Asst. Secretary of Agriculture

From the Department of Home Economics, University of Minnesota, come these successful receipts for breads in which rye, cornmeal, cottonseed flour and oatmeal are substituted for all or part of wheat flour.

Yeast Cornmeal Bread
2 tbsp. sugar
1 tbsp. fat
2 tsp. salt
1¼ c. liquid (milk and water)
½ cake compressed yeast softened in
¼ c. liquid (editor's note: substitute
½ package active dry yeast*)
⅔ c. cornmeal
1⅔ c. flour

Each of the above proportions makes 1 loaf of bread

Directions:
Add sugar, fat, and salt to liquid and bring to the boiling point. Add the cornmeal slowly, stirring constantly until all is added. Bring to the boiling point. Remove from the fire and cool. These proportions of cornmeal and water result in so thick a mixture that to add the given amounts of flour looks impossible. It can be done, however. Add yeast

dissolved in water. Add flour and knead. Let rise until about double its bulk, knead again and put in pans. When light, bake in a moderate oven (350°F) for at least an hour.

*If dried yeast is used, a sponge should be made from about ½ cupful of liquid taken from the amount given in the proportions, and some of the flour. This is allowed to rise before adding the cornmeal mixture and the remainder of the flour.

Yeast Oatmeal Bread

1 c. liquid (milk and water)
1 c. rolled oats
2 tbsp. sugar
1 tsp. salt
1 tbsp. fat
½ cake compressed yeast softened in ¼ c. liquid (editor's note: substitute ½ package active dry yeast*)
2½ c. wheat flour

This proportion makes 1 loaf of bread

Scald liquid and pour over rolled oats, sugar, salt, and fat. Let stand until lukewarm. Add yeast softened in warm water. Add flour and knead. Let rise until double in bulk. Knead again and place in pans. When light, bake 45 minutes to 1 hour in moderate oven (350°F).

Yeast Rice Bread

½ c. milk
6 tbsp. sugar
1½ tsp. salt
4 tbsp. fat
½ cake compressed yeast softened in ¼ c. liquid (editor's note: substitute ½ package active dry yeast*)
7 c. boiled rice*
8 c. flour

This proportion makes 2 loaves of bread.

Scald the milk with sugar, salt, and fat. Let cool until lukewarm and pour over the boiled rice. Add yeast and flour, and knead. Let rise until double its bulk. Knead again and put into pans. Let rise until light and bake 50 minutes to 1 hour in a moderate oven (350°F).
*The rice should be boiled in a large quantity of boiling water, in order to insure a dry rice. At least 8 or 10 times as much water as rice should be used.

Winter Wheat

By Grace Noll Crowell

THERE is a green light over the land.
In the sharp wind the bare boughs
shiver.
Huddled together the young colts stand,
And yet there is an exquisite quiver
Of pale-green light in the heady wind:
Caught in its brittleness, a flowing
Of apple-green that is sharply thinned
Where once the tawny weeds were growing.

Wheat! The Wheat! Sown long to lie
Alone beneath the snow's white drifting.
Under the gusty, wintry sky
Its sudden inch-long spears are lifting,
And soon beneath the rain and sun
The jointed stalks—the full grain bending:
A promise kept, and work well done,
And a field at rest at the summer's ending.

But here—this moment—the air is rife,
And the land is pregnant with age-old
meaning:
Here is the substance, the form of life;
Here is the hope of a golden gleaning.

❧ *Gashe* ❧

September 1928

B efore I went to Guernsey I read Victor Hugo's "Toilers of the Sea," A thrilling Channel Island story of the Guernseyman who ran the first steamboat to the French coast shortly after Fulton's Hudson trial. Whenever food is mentioned in this book the people are serving something called "gashe." If it was possible I wanted to find out what it was and how it was made. It was several days before I realized that the rich currant bread which the people called "Guernsey gosh" was the same as "gashe."

It is doubtful if many households have a written recipe for this decidedly local bread. It is one of the things that mothers have been teaching to their daughters for hundreds of years. One woman said she had a recipe and I got ready to take it down. The first thing she read was, "A pennyworth of yeast," and the last thing was, " some water." It seemed hopeless at first, but I decided to take it down and try using a cake of compressed yeast. The result was satisfactory. I've tried the following recipe and it works well.

Weigh out 1½ lbs. flour and add 1 tbsp. sugar. Dissolve 1 cake of compressed yeast (editor's note: substitute 1 package active dry yeast) in ½ c. water. Make a hole in the flour and pour in the yeast and water. Cover all of the liquid with the flour and let it rise in a warm place over night. In the morning add ½ lb. butter that has not been creamed, 1 lb. dried English currants, ¼ tsp. salt, ⅛ lb. candied lemon peel, and 1¼ c. water. Knead as you would bread and make into a loaf in a deep, round baking dish. Let it rise in a warm place for 2 hours. Bake in a moderate oven (350°F). It will take at least an hour for it to bake. For serving, Guernsey gashe is cut in three-cornered pieces the same as a pie.

170

Rolls

Rolls and Fancy Breads
1934

1 cake compressed yeast (editor's note: substitute 1 package active dry yeast)
½ c. lukewarm water
1 pt. milk, scalded
6 tbsp. shortening
4 tbsp. sugar
2 tsp. salt
7 to 8 c. flour

Dissolve yeast in water. Scald milk with shortening and sugar. Cool to lukewarm; add yeast; add about 3 c. flour and salt to make a batter. Beat until smooth. Cover and let rise about 50 minutes in a warm place, until light. Add rest of flour or enough to handle. Knead thoroughly, place in a well-greased bowl; cover and let rise until double. Make into rolls or loaf. Let rise until double in bulk and bake. Small rolls bake in 30 minutes in a fairly hot oven (400°F to 425°F); a loaf bakes in 45 minutes in a more moderate oven (375°F to 400°F).

The Staff Of Life In Other Lands

What The Pictures Tell

1. A community bake oven, used by all the villagers in a settlement in the Spreewald, Germany.

2. The staff of life in Hawaii is called poi. Here is a native pounding it in the process of making.

3. Syrian women baking bread in front of their home.

4. Women of Sardinia, Italy, baking bread.

5. Loaves in Esthonia (Russia) weigh 25 pounds. We are told that bread can be purchased more cheaply in starving Europe than it can in the United States. A purchaser can buy any portion of a 25-pound loaf.

6. An Armenian orphan and his daily ration of bread furnished by the Near East Relief.

7. Women at the mill in Palestine, the Holy Land.

8. A baker in the Sunda Islands, Malay Archipelago, carries his bakeshop on his shoulders. He has his wares displayed in a sanitary glass case.

9. A scene in what is called Old Quebec, Canada, the older portion of the historic old city. This French Canadian housekeeper is setting her bread in the outdoor oven as still is the custom in parts of France.

10. This woman bread-merchant of Paris specializes in the delivery of bread for various bakers on a monthly payment basis. She also gets her own supply of the staff of life gratis.

11. A street bread-vendor in Cairo, Egypt, where sanitary bakeries are still unknown.

12. Scene at the bread market, Harkow, China. Here the "celestials" gather for their meals, purchasing their breadsticks and moving on to nearby tables where soup and delectable Chinese dishes are served with tea.

Ice Box Rolls

1934

1 qt. milk, scalded and cooled
1 c. mashed potatoes
½ to ¾ c. sugar
¾ c. melted shortening
1 cake compressed yeast dissolved in ¼ c. luke-warm water (editor's note: substitute 1 package active dry yeast)
1 tsp. baking powder
1 tsp. baking soda
1 tbsp. salt
about 2¾ c. flour

Mix the ingredients together, adding enough flour to make a thin batter or sponge. Let it rise until it is full of bubbles. Add more flour to make a dough as stiff as would be desirable for Parker House rolls—light, fluffy, oval-shaped dinner rolls that originated at the Parker House hotel in Boston in the mid-19th century. Knead thoroughly; put in a large covered container; grease top of dough and lid together. Put in ice box for 24 hours before using. This mixture will keep for several days. When ready to use, take as much dough as desired; let it stand in a warm room for about 2 hours; make into rolls. Let rolls rise for 1 hour; bake in a hot oven (425°F) for about 20 minutes. This will make 96 small rolls.

Sweet Roll Dough

April 1938

1 c. milk, scalded
1 c. lukewarm water
2 packages active dry yeast
½ c. butter
⅔ c. sugar
1 tsp. salt
2 eggs, beaten
½ lemon, grated rind and juice
⅛ tsp. nutmeg
about 7 c. sifted flour

Scald milk and cool to lukewarm. Pour luke-warm water over yeast, stir, and let stand 10 minutes. Cream together butter, sugar, and salt, add beaten eggs, lemon juice and rind, and nut-meg. Combine milk with yeast mixture, add 3 c. flour and beat smooth. Add the butter-sugar mixture and more flour to make a soft dough. Knead smooth but keep as soft as can be han-dled without sticking. Let dough rise in a cozy warm place until doubled. Shape into rolls at once or knead down and let rise another ½ hour or so. (LN note: the rolls can be baked as is.) Or, make into cinnamon buns, butterscotch rolls (spread rolled out dough generously with butter and brown sugar, roll and cut), or pecan rolls (butterscotch rolls with a mixture of pecans, butter, and sugar in the bottom of a baking pan). Bake at 400 for 15–20 minutes (for plain rolls) and up to 25 minutes, for sugared rolls.

Mrs. C.M. [a reader-tester] in Nebraska said: "The rolls were delicious and could not be improved upon. The family thought them perfect."

174

Delicate Rolls

March 1938

1 package quick (or rapid-rise) yeast
1 tbsp. sugar
1 c. lukewarm water
1 c. milk, scalded and cooled, or lukewarm water
6 c. sifted flour
1 egg, beaten
4 to 6 tbsp. fat
3 tbsp. sugar
2 tsp. salt

Add yeast and sugar to lukewarm water, stir and let stand 10 minutes. Add cup of milk or water and ½ the flour. Beat until smooth. Add egg, softened or melted fat, sugar, salt, and rest of flour. Knead into a medium firm dough, adding more flour if necessary, until smooth and elastic. Let dough rise until doubled in a cozy place, fold or knead down and let rise ¾ as much as the first time. Fold down and divide into rolls, shaping as desired. Let rise in greased pans until double in bulk. Bake about 20 minutes in a moderately hot oven (400°F).

Mrs. L.H. [a reader-tester] from Oregon said: "The best rolls I ever made. They were as fresh and tender the next day as they were the day of baking."

Butterhorn Rolls

April 1937

1 c. milk, scalded
2 tbsp. sugar
1 c. lukewarm water
1 cake compressed yeast [editor's note: substitute 1 package active dry yeast]
7 to 8 c. sifted flour
½ c. fat
½ c. sugar
6 egg yolks
1 tbsp. salt
1 egg, beaten with 1 tbsp. cold water

Scald milk with 2 tbsp. sugar and cool to lukewarm. Add water and yeast which has been mixed with part of the water. Add 3 c. flour to make a spongy batter. Beat, let stand until light. Cream fat and sugar, add egg yolks, and beat until light and fluffy. Add to sponge with rest of flour and salt. Knead lightly and cover and let stand in warm place until double in bulk. Divide in 3 pieces, roll out each one in ⅓-inch thick rounds. Spread with soft butter, cut in 16 pie-shaped pieces. Beginning at large end, roll up each section with point at top, place on greased tin, brush top with egg beaten with water, and let stand, covered, until double in bulk. Bake 20 minutes in a hot oven (425°F).

Yeast Cakes

❧ *Perfectly Baked Bread* ❧
There Are Endless Varieties of Toothsome Dainties from Sweet Doughs

By Hanna L. Wessling, Extension Specialist, Office of Extension Work South, Washington D.C., January 1922

Dainty buns, fragrant coffee cakes, delectable tea rings and scores of other things are too often associated in our minds with the fancy bake-shop only. Comparatively few housewives realize that they may prepare these at home at relatively little cost. With some extra sugar and shortening, an egg or two, a little spice or other flavoring, and possibly some nuts or raisins, plain bread sponge or dough presents a world of wonderful possibilities. The fragrant aroma which floats from the kitchen while these goodies are baking sets everyone tingling with pleasurable anticipation. No longer will the housewife be content to shape her dough merely into plain bread, when once she realizes how easily an endless variety of good things may be evolved with which to please the family and add variety to the meals.

Nor are these products really difficult to make. The extra sugar in the dough assures good rising; the blending of various ingredients provides flavor, and the consistency of the dough may vary from that soft enough to spread to that stiff enough to roll on the board. Beating the dough until smooth and light is their chief factor in manipulation to be kept in mind by the beginner. By attempting at first only the simplest coffee cake, gradually progressing to kneaded and rolled doughs, the novice will soon develop skill sufficient to undertake the most elaborate forms desired.

Yeast Coffee Cake with Sour Cream Topping

Basic Dough:
1 cake [package] active dry yeast
2 tbsp. lukewarm water
5 tbsp. sugar
4 tbsp. shortening
1 tsp. salt
1 c. scalded milk

| 1 egg or 2 yolks |
| 3½ to 4 c. flour |

Dissolve yeast in warm water. Add sugar, shortening, and salt to scalded milk and cool. Add the egg, well beaten, and yeast, and stir in flour to make a soft dough. Let rise in a cozy place until light, about 2½ to 3 hours. Roll or pat out and fit into greased tins. This makes 2 cakes of pie-tin size or one deep 9 inch square. Let rise until nearly double, about 1 hour, and bake 30 to 40 minutes in a moderately hot oven (400°F). Finish with:

Sour Cream Topping:
Mix equal parts thick sour cream and brown sugar (About 1 c., or enough to cover). Spread on cake, pressing into indentations made in the cake with a knife handle. Sprinkle with cinnamon.

German Kuchen (Coffee Cake)
April 1938

1 package active dry yeast
¾ c. sugar
¼ c. water
3½ c. flour, sifted
1 c. milk
1 tsp. salt
1 egg
½ tsp. nutmeg
½ c. raisins
¼ c. shortening

Topping:
1½ tbsp. butter
2 tbsp. granulated sugar
1 tbsp. brown sugar
½ tsp. cinnamon, if desired

Dissolve yeast and 2 tbsp. sugar in lukewarm water. Scald milk and cool until lukewarm. Add dissolved yeast and sugar mixture. Sift flour before and after measuring. Add ½ flour and beat thoroughly. Cover, and allow sponge to rise in a warm place until full of bubbles, about 45 minutes. Add remainder of sugar, salt, slightly beaten egg, nutmeg, raisins, and melted shortening. Add remainder of flour gradually and beat thoroughly after each addition. Let stand 10 minutes. Turn onto lightly floured board and knead until smooth and elastic. Place in bowl, cover and let rise until double in size, about 1½ hrs. Shape into 2 loaves to fit greased pans. Let rise until light—about 45 minutes. For topping, spread with soft butter. Sprinkle with sugars and cinnamon. Bake in moderately hot oven (400°F) for 30 minutes. Remove from pans and allow to cool before storing.

Mrs. W.B. [a reader-tester] from Illinois: "I'm calling on some friends this afternoon and one of these coffee cakes is going along with me because I'm eager for others, too, to learn of the fine qualities of this nice product and the good work the Reader Test Department of your magazine is doing for the public. I am so enthusiastic about this entire affair that I do want you to know and feel I am 100% heart and soul in it and I'll probably be a reader of The Farmer's Wife *Magazine until I'm so old I can't read anymore."*

Thanksgiving Cake

December 1913

2 c. milk
2½ lbs. flour
8 oz. yeast
1½ lbs. sugar
10 oz. butter
10 oz. lard
1¼ lbs. raisins
1½ tsp. ground mace
1½ tsp. nutmeg
¼ c. water
1 whole egg + 1 egg yolk
Juice of 1 orange
½ c. citron, shredded

Batter should be made the night before of milk, flour, yeast, and half the sugar. In the morning, add the shortening, rest of the sugar, and the other ingredients, working well with the hands into a smooth batter. Put in well-greased pans in 4 loaves and bake in a moderately hot oven (375°F) until done.

NOW—EVEN HUSBANDS
CAN MAKE MARVELOUS BREAD THE
NEW *Speed Bake* WAY

2 MINUTES *today* SAVE
2 HOURS *tomorrow* • •

1 *MAKE YEAST FERMENT* in afternoon. Soak 1 cake yeast 20 minutes in ½ cup warm water. Pare, boil, and mash 1 potato. Mix with yeast in 1 quart lukewarm potato water (salted). 1 tablespoon sugar. Keep at 80°.

2 *NEXT MORNING,* mix 4 tablespoons sugar in yeast ferment and blend into 12 cups flour and 3 teaspoons salt. Add 4 tablespoons cooled, melted shortening.

3 *KNEAD.* Let rise in warm place until doubled. Make 4 loaves and let rise. (If hard wheat flour is used, knead and let rise *twice* before making loaves.)

4 *READY* for moderately hot oven in 4 hours or less. Bake 50 to 60 minutes—1 to 2 hours saved.

Wins 1934 First Prize With Yeast Foam

"I attribute my success in baking to this wonderful product," writes the winner of the first prize for graham bread in this year's South Dakota State Fair—Mrs. M. Eckmann.

Just the same except in name Package of five cakes at your grocer's 10c

This Sure Success Way With OVEN-TESTED Yeast Saves 1 to 2 Hours

DON'T tell him. Keep secret how very simple and sure *SPEED BAKING* is. Just accept your husband's praise for your skill as the best bread maker in all the world.

Yet the truth is this: husbands actually tested the new *SPEED BAKE* method. Even men who had never baked before, saved 2 hours over other methods. Even their clumsy hands turned out (wonder of wonders!) perfect loaves.

Best of all, *SPEED BAKING* calls for Yeast Foam or Magic Yeast—the yeast that stays fresh. It comes in *dry* cakes and yeast can't start to grow until it has been moistened. It keeps for weeks.

No wonder the *SPEED BAKE* method is changing the nation's baking habits! Try it yourself. Learn how two minutes spent today will save two hours tomorrow. Mail the coupon now for a free copy of *SPEED BAKE* recipes and a free sample of Yeast Foam.

❧ Sour Dough Bread and Biscuits ❧

By L.A.H. N., Oregon, April 1910

I often wish I knew who it was that originated sour dough bread. I guess it was some man away off on a backwoods homestead, who lighted on it by chance. Having happened to spill some flour into a little sour milk, he noticed how it worked!

The men who inhabit this half-wild land in the Oregon coast range would not dream of making any other kind of bread. It was a man who taught the art to our sons in their lonely ranch, and they swear by it still.

I have simplified the process, but I will give the other, too, as being, I conclude, more professional.

To make a start: sift a quart of flour into an earthenware jar. To this stir in as much buttermilk as will make a very thick batter. If too thin, the whey separates, and the breadmaking is more troublesome. In a warm kitchen and near the stove, it will work quickly. When it occupies more space than before, and there are small air-bubbles on the top, it is fit to use.

Take out, then, as much batter as you need, leaving always enough for a fresh start. As well as you can judge, put, say, a pint of flour, add a pinch of salt and a good pinch of baking soda. The matter of soda, depends of course, on the sourness of your dough. Observation, practice and experience alone are needed.

Stir the flour thoroughly into your bowl, if not enough to thicken it, a little more (without salt and soda) is easily added. For biscuits, you want a dough of the consistency that is used for baking powder biscuits. Have a baking pan well greased. Take up your dough by spoonfuls, and place them evenly—and not too close—in your pan; smear a little grease on the top if you like it. Bake in a quick oven (400°F) first on the bottom, and then on the top. They will divide up easily when ready for the table.

Now the man in question, spreads his mixed dough onto the pastry board, rolls it out about ¾ of an inch thick, cuts it with a biscuit cutter, and places the pieces quite close together in the pan. He greases the top generously, and lets them rise a little before placing in the oven. Of course they come out a uniform shape, but the crust is not so nice.

I have never measured the quantity of dough used, being I suppose, like the Irish woman who said she measured everything by "fistfuls." However, I have done so now, and I find that I take about a quart and a half of dough from the jar.

For a loaf, a quart would be enough. To this add the flour, salt and soda. Only make a stiffer dough—as stiff as required for yeast bread. When mixed, continue cutting it with a spoon, and turning it over, as does the mechanical bread-mixer.

With a little flour on your hand, it is easy to turn it out onto a greased pan. Place it in a warm place near the stove, to rise. When well risen, bake in a moderate oven (350°F) with as crisp and thick a crust as you prefer.

Now the man and my son (because the man taught him), faithfully kneaded their dough, with floury hands, before putting it to rise. Nobody could detect that all that extra trouble had been taken. To "perpetuate the race" in your dough jar to what you left, add a sifter of flour, and as much sweet milk as you find necessary, stirring it well. The flour of course, must be in proportion to your requirements.

For the next morning's use, it rises well in a moderate temperature. Should your milk run short, a little water can be substituted. It does not do to have sour dough bread now and then only. You will find it will turn "rotten" in the jar, if neglected too long.

As now-a-days, scientific doctors are crying up the beneficial effects of sour milk [buttermilk]. I can but believe it makes not only a palatable, but wholesome bread also. The pinch of soda does not neutralize everything.

The jar needs to be scrubbed clean every day, above where the dough ends. The bread keeps well, and some people prefer it a day or two old. I have been experimenting lately on using it with shortening and sugar in different ways.

Quick Breads and Muffins

Quick breads are mixed and baked quickly. They depend upon baking powder or soda, or a combination of the two, or steam, as leavening agents. Light handling and quick mixing help spell success. That common fault, excess of soda or baking powder, can be avoided if one is familiar with the rules for their use. Muffins should be stirred up in a hurry - it is a one, two, three, and then pop them in the oven.

1. Mix together all the dry ingredients.
2. Mix together all the wet ingredients.
3. Combine the two mixtures.

Quick Breads

"With a Cornish Flavor"

"Currany 'Obbin"
September 1932

Make a stiffish paste with flour and lard and a pinch of salt, not no baking powder. Wet it up with milk if you got it, water if you ab'n got it. Roll it out nice and thin and sprinkle it over with currans, nice and thick. Then roll it up careful like you would your starch clothes, squeeze home the ends and brush it over with the white of an egg if you want it to shine. Them clap 'em in the ob'n. The children so dearly like it, and they say currans be full of the new fangled "vitamines" the Doctors be always ordering, they ought to be good for 'em.

P.S.: If you get tired of currans you can make a "figgy" wan fer a change.

P.P.S's: Figs is just Cornish for raisins.

—*St. Kea, Wisconsin*

Quick Graham Bread

February 1932

2 c. graham flour
½ c. white flour
5 tsp. baking powder
1 tsp. salt
4 tbsp. melted fat
1½ c. milk
½ c. molasses or ⅓ c. sugar
½ c. nutmeats

Mix and sift flours, baking powder, and salt. Then add fat, milk, molasses, and nutmeats. Turn into buttered bread pan and bake 45 to 50 minutes in moderately hot oven (400°F).

Buckwheat, Raisin, and Nut Bread

February 1918

1 c. rye flour
1 c. buckwheat flour
½ tsp. baking soda
2 tsp. baking powder
½ tsp. salt
½ c. brown sugar
1 c. milk
1 egg (may be omitted)

Mix the flours, soda, baking powder, and salt. Dissolve the sugar in the milk and add the egg, if egg is to be used. Combine the flour and milk mixtures. Bake in a very moderate oven (300°F) for 1 hour. Chopped nuts or raisins or currants may be added to this bread to give variety.

Date Bread

June 1928

1½ c. white flour, measured after sifting
4 tsp. baking powder
1½ tsp. salt
1½ c. graham or whole wheat flour
½ c. brown sugar
1 c. sliced dates
1 c. coarsely chopped nuts
1½ c. milk
¼ c. molasses

Mix together the white flour, baking powder, and salt, add the graham flour and the brown sugar. Then add the dates and nuts. Stir in the milk and finally the molasses. Beat thoroughly and bake in a greased loaf pan in a slow oven (300°F) for about 1 hour. This makes 1 loaf, moist but not sticky.

Prune Nut Bread

August 1933

1 c. honey
¼ c. fat
¼ c. brown sugar
3 eggs
3 tsp. salt
2 c. cornmeal
1½ c. whole wheat flour
2½ c. white flour
7 tsp. baking powder
1 tsp. baking soda
2 c. nut meats
1 c. mashed prunes
2½ c. milk

Cream honey, fat, and brown sugar. Add beaten eggs. Combine all dry ingredients, add to first mixture. Then add mashed prunes and milk. When mixed, divide batter and bake in 2 greased loaf pans. Bake 1 hour and 15 minutes in moderate oven (325°F). Makes 2 loaves.

Peanut Butter Bread I

December 1932

2 c. whole wheat flour
1 tsp. salt
½ tsp. baking soda
1½ tsp. baking powder
½ c. peanut butter
1 c. buttermilk
1 egg

Mix and sift the dry ingredients, rub in the peanut butter. Add the beaten egg to the buttermilk and combine the mixtures. It should be a thick batter. Grease baking powder or coffee can well (editor's note: or a loaf pan), fill ⅔ full, let stand 15 minutes and bake in a moderately hot oven (400°F).

Peanut Butter Bread II
November 1934

2 c. bread flour
⅓ c. sugar
2 tsp. baking powder
1 tsp. salt
¾ c. peanut butter
1 egg, beaten
1 c. milk

Sift dry ingredients together. Work in peanut butter with a fork or dough blender, add egg and milk to make a soft dough. Pour in greased loaf pan. Bake 50 to 60 minutes in a moderate oven (375°F).

—*Iowa State College*

Fig Whole Wheat Bread
June 1928

2 c. whole wheat or graham flour
1 tsp. baking soda
1 tsp. salt
1 c. bread flour
3 tsp. baking powder
⅓ c. brown sugar
½ c. chopped nut meats
1 c. dried figs, cut very fine
½ c. molasses
½ c. water
¾ c. milk
2 tbsp. melted shortening

Mix the dry ingredients, add the nuts and figs. Combine the molasses, water, milk, and shortening and stir into the first mixture. Pour into a greased bread pan and let stand for 20 minutes. Bake slowly (300°F) for about 1 hour.

Apricot Nut Bread

September 1934

1½ c. dried apricots
2 tbsp. shortening
½ c. sugar
1 egg
1 c. sweet milk
2½ c. flour
3¼ tsp. baking powder
½ tsp. salt
¼ tsp. baking soda
½ c. chopped nuts

Wash apricots. Cover with water and boil 5 minutes. Drain, cool, and chop. Cream shortening and sugar, add well-beaten egg. Add apricots and milk, then gradually the sifted dry ingredients and nuts. Bake in a greased loaf pan 1 hour at 350°F.

—*C.E., Illinois*

Honey Orange Bread

June 1928

rind of 3 oranges
1 c. honey
¼ c. water
3 c. flour, measured after sifting
4 tsp. baking powder
1 c. chopped nuts
1 egg
1 c. milk

Save the rind from three fine, thick-skinned oranges, cut in very small strips, and boil in salted water for about a half hour or until tender. Pour off the water and boil the orange strips again, very slowly, in the honey and water until very thick.

Sift together the dry ingredients and add the nuts. Beat the egg, add the milk, then the orange and honey mixture. Stir the liquid into the dry ingredients.

Pour into a greased pan and bake for an hour in a slow oven (300°F).

Plain Walnut Bread

June 1928

3 c. flour, measured after sifting
¾ c. brown sugar
½ tsp. salt
3 tsp. baking powder
½ c. walnuts
½ c. raisins
1 egg
1 c. milk or buttermilk

Mix and sift the dry ingredients. Add the walnut meats and raisins. Beat the egg and add to it the milk, and stir all into the flour mixture. Pour into a greased pan and bake for an hour in a slow oven (300°F).

Tea Bread

October 1927

2 c. whole wheat flour
½ tsp. salt
¼ c. sugar
3 tsp. baking powder
½ c. peanut butter
¾ c. chopped dates or raisins
1 c. milk

Mix dry ingredients, rub in peanut butter, add fruit, and stir in milk. Pour into small greased bread pan and bake in moderate oven (350°F) about 1 hour.

Banana Loaf
March 1939

1 c. sugar
¼ c. fat
1 egg
3 mashed bananas
2 c. sifted flour
1 tsp. baking soda
½ tsp. salt
1 c. nut meats

Cream sugar and fat, add egg and bananas and blend well. Sift together dry ingredients, add nuts and combine with the batter. Stir just until flour is dampened, put in greased loaf pan. Bake 1 hour in very moderate oven (350°F).

—*Mrs. E. O. Park*

Chocolate Nut Loaf
March 1933

2½ c. cake flour
1/4 tsp. salt
1 tsp. baking soda
1 c. butter
2 c. sugar
3 eggs, well beaten
1 c. walnut meats, coarsely broken
3 squares unsweetened chocolate, melted
1 c. buttermilk
2 tsp. vanilla

Sift flour once, measure, add salt and baking soda and sift together 3 times. Cream butter thoroughly, add sugar gradually, and cream together until light and fluffy. Add eggs and beat well. Add nuts and chocolate and blend. Add flour mixture, alternately with buttermilk, a small amount at a time, beating after each addition until smooth. Add vanilla. Bake in greased loaf pan in slow oven (325°F) for 1 hour, or until done.

Sally Lunn

March 1934

3 tbsp. butter
⅓ c. sugar
2 eggs
2 c. sifted flour
2 tsp. baking powder
½ tsp. salt
1 c. milk

Cream butter and sugar together, add well beaten eggs. Alternately add sifted dry ingredients and milk. Beat, pour into a greased loaf pan. Bake in a moderately hot oven (400°F). Cut in squares to serve. A traditional accompaniment in some families is whipped cream (very slightly sweetened if at all) in place of butter.

Some of the older recipes call for yeast as the leavening agent and the batter, when light, is baked in gem pans or a tube pan.

Seed Cake

September 1928

¾ lb. flour
6 oz. sugar
6 oz. butter
3 eggs
3 tsp. baking powder
¼ tsp. salt
¼ c. caraway seeds
½ c. water

The material is mixed together in the order listed. This cake is baked in a round deep dish. Baking requires about an hour in a moderate oven (350°F).

White Loaf Cake

January 1914

Cream ½ c. butter with 1½ c. sugar. Add 1 c. milk, 1½ c. flour, 2 tsp. baking powder, beaten whites of 5 eggs, ¼ tsp. almond extract, and ½ tsp. orange extract.

By thoroughly beating the mixture before the whites of the eggs are added, a delicate fine-grained cake will be had. Bake in a buttered loaf tin, in a moderate oven (350°F). Ice this cake with Allegretti Icing (page 104).

Orange Cake

January 1914

⅓ c. butter
grated rind of 1 orange (orange part only)
1 c. powdered sugar
2 eggs, separated
1½ c. sifted pastry flour
1 rounded tsp. baking powder
½ c. milk

Cream the butter and add the grated orange rind, beat in gradually ½ c. powdered sugar, then the well beaten yolks of 2 eggs mixed with the second ½ c. sugar. Sift together the flour and baking powder 3 to 4 times, then add the flour to the mixture alternately with ½ c. milk. Lastly, add the whites of the eggs beaten very dry. Bake in a moderate oven (350°F) in a buttered loaf tin. Ice with Orange Icing (page 105).

Basic Honey Cake

August 1933

½ c. shortening
½ c. honey
½ c. sugar
2 eggs
2 c. cake flour
3 tsp. baking powder
¼ tsp. salt
⅓ c. milk
2 tsp. cream

Cream shortening, honey, and sugar. Add beaten eggs and beat until thoroughly blended. Sift dry ingredients together and add alternately with milk to honey mixture. Do not beat after all flour has been incorporated, just 2 or 3 stirs to be sure it is well blended. Add the cream, stir, and pour into a well-greased loaf pan. Bake in moderate oven (350°F) for about 50 minutes.

Pound Cakes

German Pound Cake

April 1937

1 c. butter or half other fat
2 c. sugar
1 lemon, juice and grated rind
10 egg yolks (or enough to make ⅔ c.)
3 c. sifted flour
1 tsp. salt
3 tsp. baking powder
1 c. milk
1 c. seedless raisins
1½ c. pecans, cut

Cream fat very thoroughly, add sugar gradually so mixture is very fluffy. Add lemon juice and rind then egg yolks, two or three at a time, unbeaten, mixing until light and creamy. Add sifted dry ingredients alternately with milk, then fruit and nuts dusted with a little of the flour. Use a greased tube pan, lining the bottom with waxed paper. Bake in a slow oven (325°F) for 1 hour. Cool in pan before removing. If nuts and raisins are omitted, it makes an excellent plain pound cake.

This lovely all-over flower-and-leaf design—the Shalimar—is adapted from an ancient Persian print

Old Fashioned Pound Cake

March 1938

1¼ c. butter
2 c. fine granulated sugar
8 eggs
2 tbsp. brandy
1 tsp. mace or nutmeg
1¾ c. sifted cake flour
1 tsp. salt
¼ tsp. baking powder

Cream butter very thoroughly and add sugar gradually. Cream together until light and fluffy. Add 1 egg at a time without separating, and beat after the addition of each egg. Add brandy and spice. Add sifted dry ingredients and beat until light and fluffy. Bake in a well greased tube pan in a very slow oven (300°F) for 1¼ hours. The heat should be turned off the last ¼ hour of baking. Pound cake is not usually iced. Store in the pan in which it is baked.

Honey Pound Cake

February 1938

2 c. flour
1 tsp. baking powder
½ c. butter
½ c. honey
4 eggs, separated
½ c. sugar
1 tsp. vanilla

Sift flour, measure, add baking powder, and sift 4 times. Cream butter very thoroughly, add honey and mix until very light and fluffy. Add 1 egg yolk at a time, blending well after each and beat 4 minutes. Beat egg whites until stiff but not dry, add sugar gradually to make a smooth meringue, and vanilla. Fold into batter, pour in a greased wax-paper-lined loaf pan (5x9 inches). Bake in a very moderate oven (325°F) for 1 hour, 10 minutes. Fine-grained, moist, a good keeping pound cake of delicate flavor.

With electric mixer, use medium speed to cream butter for 1 minute and mix in honey for 5 minutes; slow speed for beating in yolks for 5 minutes; medium speed for meringue and slow to fold it in.

Muffins

Bran Muffins

October 1927

2 tbsp. shortening
¼ c. sugar
1 egg
1 c. bran
1 c. flour
½ tsp. salt
½ tsp. baking soda
1 tsp. baking powder
1 c. buttermilk

Cream together shortening and sugar, add egg and bran. Add flour sifted with other dry ingredients and buttermilk. If sweet milk is used, omit baking soda and use 2 tsp. baking powder. Bake 20 minutes in moderate oven (375°F).

Buckwheat Muffins

May 1918

1 tsp. salt
4 tsp. baking powder
1 c. wheat flour
⅞ c. buckwheat flour
1 tbsp. fat
1 tbsp. maple syrup
1 egg
1 c. milk

Sift dry materials together. Add the melted fat, syrup, and beaten egg to the milk. Combine these 2 mixtures, stirring lightly without beating. Bake about 30 minutes in a moderately hot oven (375°F).

Rye Muffins

December 1913

2 c. rye flour. To this add 1 c. white flour, 2 c. buttermilk, ¼ c. molasses, 1 tsp. baking soda, ½ tsp. salt, 1 tsp. shortening. Place in buttered muffin tins and bake in a quick oven (400°F).

Whole Wheat Muffins

October 1927

2 c. whole wheat flour
3 tsp. baking powder
½ tsp. salt
2 tbsp. sugar
1 egg
1 c. milk
1 tbsp. melted butter

Mix together dry ingredients. Beat egg slightly and mix with milk and melted butter. Add all dry ingredients at one time to liquid to prevent lumping. Pour into greased muffin pans and bake in medium oven (375°F) about 25 minutes. Increase heat if necessary for browning during the last 10 minutes.

Sweet Whole Wheat Muffins

October 1927

2 c. whole wheat flour
¾ tsp. salt
¾ tsp. baking soda
1 egg
½ c. molasses
¾ c. milk

Mix together dry ingredients. Beat egg slightly and mix with molasses and milk. Add all dry ingredients at one time to liquid to prevent lumping. Pour into greased muffin pans and bake in medium oven (375°F) about 25 minutes. Increase heat if necessary for browning during the last 10 minutes.

Sour Milk Muffins

April 1912

1½ c. flour, ½ tsp. baking soda, ¼ tsp. salt, 1 c. buttermilk. Sift the dry ingredients together, add the buttermilk lightly. Bake ½ hour at 375°F in buttered muffin tins.

❀ The Patriotic Potato— ❀
Use It in Place of Bread in the Meals to Eke Out Wheat Flour in Your Receipts
From the United States Food Administrations

May 1918

A large supply of potatoes is on hand. They must be used or go to waste. Now is the time to use them while the ban on meat is lifted for a while. Back up savory stews with ample servings of potatoes to cut down on bread.

Potatoes are an acceptable substitute for bread. A pound of baked potatoes is equal in nutritive value to 7 ounces of bread. Join the "Wheat Savers League." Use the perishable potato as a wheat and as a bread substitute.

Potato Muffins
4 tbsp. fat
2 tbsp. sugar
1 egg
1 c. mashed potato
2 c. flour
3 tbsp. baking powder
½ tsp. salt
1 c. milk

Cream the fat and sugar; add the egg, well beaten; then the potato and mix thoroughly. Sift flour, baking powder, and salt; add milk and flour alternately. Bake in greased muffin tins 25 to 30 minutes at 250°F.

Potato Biscuit
1 c. flour
4 tsp. baking powder
1 tsp. salt
2 tbsp. fat
1 c. mashed potato
½ c. water or milk (about)

Sift together flour, baking powder, and salt; work in the fat with fork or knife. Add potato and mix thoroughly. Then add enough liquid to make a soft dough. Roll the dough lightly to about ½ inch in thickness; cut into biscuits and bake 12 to 15 minutes in hot oven (400°F).

Tea Muffins

October 1927

1 c. dry breadcrumbs
1 c. milk
1 egg
2 tbsp. melted fat
½ c. molasses
1½ c. whole wheat flour
½ tsp. salt
½ tsp. baking soda
3 tsp. baking powder
½ tsp. cinnamon
½ tsp. nutmeg
¼ tsp. ground cloves

Soften the breadcrumbs in milk, and add egg, slightly beaten, melted fat, and molasses. Mix dry ingredients and add at one time to other mixture. Bake about 25 minutes in medium oven (375°F), in greased muffin tins.

Cornmeal Tea Cakes

January 1910

1 c. cornmeal; 2 eggs; 2 c. flour; 1½ c. buttermilk; 2 c. sugar; 4 tbsp. lard; 1 tsp. each baking soda, salt, and lemon extract. Bake in muffin tins in a quick oven (400°F). Serve while hot.

Mammy's Corn Bread

March 1921

1 c. cornmeal
1 c. flour
1 tbsp. sugar
1 tsp. baking soda
1 tsp. salt
buttermilk (approximately 1½ c.)
1 egg

Sift well together. Then work in 1 tbsp. shortening. Mix to a medium batter with buttermilk. Whip in 1 well-beaten egg and bake in a hot oven (400°F).

Cocoa Muffins

March 1921

3 tbsp. unsweetened cocoa
½ c. boiling water
1½ tsp. baking powder
¼ tsp. salt
1¼ c. flour
2 eggs, separated
2 tbsp. melted butter
¾ c. sugar

Dissolve the cocoa in the boiling water. Mix the baking powder, salt, and flour. Separate the eggs, beat the yolks slightly. Mix the butter and sugar together, add beaten yolks, the dissolved cocoa, then the flour mixture and lastly fold in the whites of eggs beaten until stiff. Bake in well-greased muffin pans in a moderate oven (350°F) for 25 minutes.

Peanut Butter Muffins

November 1934

2 c. sifted flour
2 tsp. baking powder
¾ tsp. salt
¼ c. sugar
4 tbsp. fat
½ c. peanut butter
1 c. milk
2 eggs, beaten

Put dry ingredients in sifter and sift into bowl. Cut in fat and peanut butter with a dough blender or sharp-tined fork. Combine milk and eggs, add to dry ingredients and stir until barely moistened. Drop in greased muffin tins and bake in a moderately hot oven (400°F) about 25 minutes. This makes 12 large muffins.

Cranberry Muffins

November 1933

2 c. flour
2½ tsp. baking powder
½ tsp. salt
2 tbsp. sugar
½ c. ground cranberries
1 c. milk
1 egg, beaten
2 tbsp. melted butter

Sift flour, baking powder, salt, and sugar together, then add cranberries. Add beaten egg to milk, then melted shortening. Beat liquids together. Add liquid to dry ingredients all at once. Combine in about 3 seconds, mixing until ingredients are just dampened. Fill greased muffin tins a little over ⅓ full. Bake in hot oven (400°F) about 20 minutes.

Blueberry Muffins

August 1923

3 tbsp. butter
½ c. sugar
2 eggs
1½ c. flour (sifted)
3 tsp. baking powder
½ tsp. salt
1 c. milk
1 c. blueberries

Cream butter, add sugar and well-beaten eggs. Mix and sift flour, baking powder, and salt, reserving a small amount of flour to dust over berries. Add flour mixture and milk alternately to butter mixture. Stir in berries last, being careful not to crush them. Bake in a moderately hot oven (400°F).

Other Quick Breads

Scotch Scones

March 1933

2 c. flour
2 tsp. baking powder
2 tsp. sugar
¾ tsp. salt
4 tbsp. butter
2 eggs
⅓ c. milk (approx.)

Sift together flour, baking powder, sugar, and salt. Work in the butter. Save out a small amount of egg white. Beat the rest of the 2 eggs and add to milk and beat again. Add to the dry ingredients and mix lightly and quickly. Toss on floured board, roll out to 1 inch in thickness and cut in triangles with a knife. Brush with the saved egg white, sprinkle with sugar and bake in a very hot oven (450°F) from 10 to 15 minutes. This makes a nicely glossed scone. They also may be cut out in squares and folded over to form 3-cornered shapes if you prefer.

—*B.W., Massachusetts*

Sago Scones

December 1913

Editor's note: Sago is a light starch obtained from sago palms. It is occasionally available at health and specialty stores. Measurements and instructions from the Farmer's Wife for this recipe are imprecise, and contemporary recipes involving sago are extremely rare. Try this as a curiosity, if you wish.

Take 1 c. sago and soak in cold water, put it on the stove with 1 quart sweet milk, let it boil till quite dissolved, stirring occasionally; add a little salt, then pour out on the baking board and let it lie till cold. Mix up with flour, taking care not to make it too stiff; roll out quite thin, cut to the size wanted and bake in a very hot oven (450°F).

Parkin

December 1913

1¾ lbs. flour, ½ lb. oatmeal, 6 tsp. baking powder, 1 tsp. ground ginger, 4 oz. butter, 2 lbs. molasses, 1 c. milk. Mix the dry ingredients well together, warm the molasses with milk and butter (do not make it hot) and mix the whole. Bake in a well-buttered tin for 1 hour at 350°F. Cut into squares before taking out of the tin. It should be 1½ inches thick.

Quick Coffee Cake

November 1932

1 egg
½ c. sugar
3 tbsp. melted unsalted butter
1 tsp. vanilla
2 tsp. baking powder
1½ c. flour
¼ tsp. salt
½ c. milk

Beat egg, add sugar, continue beating; gradually beat in shortening. Add vanilla. Sift baking powder and flour together, add salt. Add milk and flour alternately to egg mixture, beginning with a little flour. Bake in a 9 or 10 inch pan. Sprinkle the following on top and bake in a moderate oven (350°F): 2 tbsp. sugar mixed with 1 tsp. cinnamon. Dot generously with butter. Brown sugar is good. Serve warm for luncheon or supper. It is good with preserves and sauce. It is extra delicious if ½ c. chopped nuts, raisins, or dates is added.

—*E.D., Minnesota*

Orange Rolls

December 1932

2 c. flour
2 tsp. baking powder
½ tsp. salt
1 tbsp. shortening
1 egg
½ c. milk
1 c. unsalted, creamed butter
12 sections orange pulp

Sift flour, baking powder, and salt together; add shortening, mixing with a fork. Beat egg slightly and add with milk to first mixture. Roll into an oblong piece about ¼ inch thick. Cut into 3-inch circles; spread with creamed butter and place a section of fresh orange coated with granulated sugar over half the circle. Fold over other half to completely cover orange and pinch edges together. Place rolls in greased baking pan and bake in moderate oven (350°F) about 20 minutes. Just before removing, brush tops with melted butter.

Uncle Sam's War Receipt for Biscuit

October 1917

2 c. white flour
2 c. cornmeal, ground soy beans or finely ground peanuts, rice flour, or other substitute
2 tsp. salt
4 tsp. baking powder
4 tbsp. shortening
liquid to mix to proper consistency (editor's note: 1 to 1½ c. milk, skim milk, or water)

Sift together twice the flour, meal, salt, and baking powder. Have the shortening as cold as possible and cut it into the mixture with a knife, finally rubbing it in with the hands. Mix quickly with the cold liquid forming a fairly soft dough which can be rolled out on the board. Turn on to a floured board; roll into a sheet not over ½ inch thick; cut into rounds, place these in lightly floured biscuit tins [or shallow pans] and bake 10 to 12 minutes in a rather hot oven (450°F). If peanuts are used, the roasted and shelled nuts should be crushed with a rolling pin.

In making the flour and peanut biscuit, the flour and other dry ingredients should be sifted together twice and then mixed thoroughly with the crushed peanuts.

Savories

❧ *Popovers* ❧

By Miriam J. Williams, November 1936

St. Paul is a popover city, no doubt about it.

Out-of-town visitors, lunching at hotels and clubs, comment on the popularity of this crispy, puffed-up bread, usually passed around piping hot on a napkin-covered server by a special waiter. Popover fans keep a speculative eye upon the size of the pile under its snowy covering, as they proceed with their Russian salad or luncheon plate. Even the dirt-watchful ones throw caution—suppose we say under the table—as they beckon for more butter, please. While women seem to be especially enthusiastic in praise of popovers, their popularity with men is proven by their inclusion as a regular luncheon stand-by at two well-known men's clubs.

St. Paul Popovers

November 1936

4 eggs, beaten slightly
1 c. milk
1 c. water
2⅓ c. sifted bread flour
1 tsp. salt
2 tsp. sugar

To eggs add ⅔ of liquid, then all of flour, salt, and sugar. (That's right, there's no baking powder.) Beat until smooth, add rest of liquid. When blended, pour in warm, thoroughly greased pans. Fill muffin pans half full, deep custard cups or popover pan scarcely more than ⅓ full. Bake smaller tins, as muffin pans, for 25 to 30 minutes, deeper tins for 35 minutes at 450°F to 475°F, a really hot oven. Serve piping hot with butter. The popovers will pop up in 15 or 20 minutes, and the additional baking makes the thin walls crisp and brown. Serve as breakfast or hot supper bread. On occasion, fill with creamed chicken or chipped beef in cream.

Pop-Overs

1934

1 c. flour
¼ tsp. salt
1 c. milk
2 eggs, unbeaten
1 tsp. melted fat

Put flour in a bowl, make a well in the center, drop in the salt. Add milk gradually and stir well. When smooth, add the unbeaten eggs and fat and beat until smooth. Fill pans ⅓ full. Bake in hissing hot muffin pans or hot earthenware or glass cups in a hot oven (450°F) about 30 minutes, then in a more moderate oven (350°F) about 15 minutes longer. Serve at once. Makes eight. Pop-overs, when properly baked, have a mostly crisp outer shell and only a very little moist material inside. Pop-overs may be split and filled with dried beef gravy or creamed chicken for a special supper dish.